There's Moore to Life

Robert Moore

Robert Moore

2011

705-329-0507

Library and Archives Canada Cataloguing in Publication

CIP data on file with the National Library and Archives

ISBN 978-0-9869152-0-8

Disclaimer and Terms of Use: The Author and Publisher has strived to be as accurate and complete as possible in the creation of this book, notwithstanding the fact that he does not warrant or represent at any time that the contents within are accurate due to the rapidly changing nature of the Internet. While all attempts have been made to verify information provided in this publication, the Author and Publisher assumes no responsibility for errors, omissions, or contrary interpretation of the subject matter herein. Any perceived slights of specific persons, peoples, or organizations are unintentional. In practical advice books, like anything else in life, there are no guarantees of income made. Readers are cautioned to reply on their own judgment about their individual circumstances to act accordingly. This book is not intended for use as a source of legal, business, accounting or financial advice. All readers are advised to seek services of competent professionals in legal, business, accounting, and finance field.

Dedications to:

In dedication I truly dedicate this book to my late common-law wife, Penny Bryck (the mother of my children), as she always said that I was much more capable of becoming a better person, although at the time I couldn't see it myself.

Lastly, I want to dedicate this book to everyone reading it who ultimately desires to become the better person they could become. Life will throw things at us that we might or might not like but it's up to us to accept it either negatively (feeling sorry for ourselves) or positively, which will allow us to become emotionally stronger.

There's Moore to Life

Table of Contents

Preface

I was in recovery for drugs and alcohol abuse; I started to sponsor people coming into recovery. While helping them face the fears I did when I was new, I felt the need to share my experience, strength and hope.

I started to do motivational speaking and someone came up to me and suggested I write a book to share with the people I can't reach. This is when the light bulb struck and I started to write my autobiography.

The process in writing this book has been very challenging, as I am a full-time student and given the fact that I had to relive all the emotions I had lived before, but this time I knew what to do while feeling them again.

Note from Author:

I have asked several people that came across my path to write their own thoughts of how they saw the way I was through their own eyes. I asked my parents, friends, even some professional people, like a retired sergeant of the Ontario Provincial Police, my Uncle Tim, who worked as a correctional officer at the Maplehurst Correctional Facility in Milton, and a probation officer who is also one of my editors for this book.

I want to show the readers that it really did happen and hopefully be able to give them hope in their own struggles they may be facing.

I wish you all the best in whatever you choose to do in your life, and I hope if anything my autobiography will help one out of fifty people who read it either emotionally, physically, or mentally.

Robert Moore

Testimonials

Arnie & Dianne Moore (Biological father and stepmom)

My name is Dianne Moore. I am the stepmother of Robert and his brother Thomas. Robert is the youngest. I also have a son, Jayson, from a previous marriage that was raised with both Robert and Thomas.

I moved in with Robert and Thomas's father, Arnie, in 1974. Robert was two years old both Thomas and Jayson where three years old. Arnie had full custody of Robert and Thomas, as I did for Jayson.

Robert was a very shy, reserved and sometimes destructive child, but he was still lovable. Arnie got full custody of the two boys; their mother, Shirley, had visitations on holidays and every other weekend. Shirley would not show up most of the time, which was very hard on the Robert and his brother. Thomas was her favourite. Robert would always come home hurt, bruised and dirty.

In school Robert had a very difficult time; things did not come to him easy at all. He was in trouble all the time, but did manage to get through it.

Arnie and I have bought a house up north in Flesherton, Ontario, when the boys were in their teen years. Figuring they wouldn't get in so much trouble in a smaller community but it seemed to be downhill from the time we moved to Flesherton, when Robert was 14. Robert seemed to have fallen apart, as it was a century shock to move to a small town of only 300 people. So Robert always said he was going to move out at the age of 16.

When Arnie and I went to pick up both Robert and Thomas from their mother's in Oakville, Ontario, Robert wasn't around. He ran away so he wouldn't have to go back up north.

When I contacted the school to let them know Robert wasn't going to come back to the school, I found out that he had been suspended for three weeks and he had to sign papers to say that when he was 16, which worked out to be the three week period of his suspension. Robert would be terminated from the school and not allowed on the school property. If he did, he could be charged with trespassing. We never did find out why or what he did.

Robert seemed to have a pattern of phoning us when he was drinking or high on drugs, or when he was in jail. While he was drunk or high he would call and we would have numerous telephone conversations along with verbal fights. It seemed that he wasn't ready to hear what we had to say about his lifestyle. It was Robert's way or no way at all.

When he had his children I thought he would change his ways, but he didn't. When Penny, the mother of his children, passed away just after she gave birth to their second child, Robert went further into himself and became angrier at everything in his way. This was the same thing when his brother, Thomas, and cousin, Timothy, were killed in car crashes.

Years later, Robert took everyone by surprise when he told everyone he was in a treatment centre to get help for his addictions, although we had heard this story way too many times. He seemed to have woken up this time and saw the light because he has done a 100% turnaround. He stopped drinking, using drugs, even smoking cigarettes, and he hasn't visited the jails again unless he was volunteering.

I believe it has been a long, hard battle for him. I am sure it will be for a long time, but Robert has made it this far, just over five years without any drugs or booze. He has upgraded his education and decided to continue until he receives his master's degree.

Robert's father and I are very proud of all his achievements, as Robert has a lot of awards and he continues to achieve more. He has gotten so many awards for volunteering through the community and helping people that it became a way of life for him.

Arnie and I will stand behind Robert all the way.

Dianne Moore

I'm Robert Moore's aunt. His father is my brother. I remember Rob as a happy baby with great big smile and dimples. He appeared to be an easygoing child. When he was a little over a year, his mother left his father. Worried how he would manage to work and look after two boys, Arnie asked if I could help him out. Since I just separated from my husband I agreed to do so. So my son Tim, who was four, and I moved in. I remained there for a few months then suggested my brother get a nanny, which he did. While I was there the boys were great kids. Nothing seemed to bother Robert, except when I was leaving to go home, and he cried and screamed. I would visit my brother on weekends to stay in touch with the boys so they wouldn't think I left them too. Then my brother was reunited with his ex-girlfriend, Dianne. Dianne later moved in with them, along with her son, Jayson.

When Rob started school he began to get into trouble, and this was kindergarten. The teacher would send him to the coatroom (timeout) to sit and think about his behaviour and there he would cut the coats with scissors. That was the beginning for Rob, and as I understood he continued to be a troubled boy.

When Robert was in his early teens the family moved up north to the country, Flesherton, Ontario, a population of 300 people. This was very hard on all the boys; there was nothing out there for them to do, so they all got in trouble. For a few summers my brother Arnie would send all three of them down to me in Mississauga because there wasn't any employment up north. I gave them two weeks to get a job or back to the boondocks. Rob was the youngest and I was a little worried about him, but for some reason these boys always obeyed me when I talked to them. My son Tim got Rob in the A&P warehouse in Toronto, where he worked the whole summer without any incidents. At the end of summer they would go back home. School started again, and the trouble would start again.

The next thing I know all the boys left home. My brother would tell me about the problems Rob would get into and end up in jail. My heart would ache for him. He continued the lifestyle of drugs, alcohol and jail. At times he would get into altercations and end up in the hospital with stab wounds. He would call me from jail and we would talk for a while about his behaviour in hoping something would sink in. Then in 1991 he became a father of a little girl, Elizabeth, but he was unable to be at her birth because he was in jail again.

When he got out I was hoping he would change his ways, now being a father, but that didn't happen. Then, in 1991, my son, Tim, was killed in a car accident. He and the three boys were very close cousins, but once again Rob was in jail and could not attend the funeral. On the first anniversary of Tim's departure, Rob, Penny and Elizabeth came to my home. Penny was eight months pregnant with their second child, Jeffrey. This was the first time I met her and saw Elizabeth since she was born. A couple of weeks later I get a call that Penny had the baby and Penny had passed away. My brother and sister-in-law came down to my home to stay a while. We went to the hospital to see the baby (later called Jeffrey) and for support for Rob. The social worker at the hospital said they would not release the baby to Rob unless he had someone to watch over him, and since my brother was going on holidays, there wasn't anyone except me, so I took them both home with me.

Rob stayed with me for about two weeks, then took Elizabeth and went back to Burlington, leaving the baby, Jeffrey, with me. There he started his bad behaviour over again and eventually had Elizabeth taken away from him. So to keep the baby safe from Rob coming and taking him in one of his drug or drunken moods, I went for custody of Jeffrey; at least I knew he wouldn't end up in Children's Aid.

Rob continued his bad behaviour, in and out of jail for sometime. He would call me to see how Jeffrey was and at times wanted to speak to him. Now I had to show tough love for Rob to see that I mean what I say, and he knew when I said I was going to do something, I followed through with it. I told him as long as he continued this lifestyle, I would not let him see or speak to his son Jeffrey, and that hurt me very much. No matter what Rob was doing with his life, I loved him dearly and I never had a problem in telling him that. When he got out of one of his jail stays he called to say he was staying in Hamilton for a while and that he had a job and was going to try and change his ways. Unfortunately, that didn't last long, his brother Tom was killed in a car accident and that started Rob's behaviour all over again. Once again he would call me and we would talk a lot. I would send him money to buy whatever in jail plus we wrote a lot as well.

Then there was a period I didn't hear from him, and

when I did he told me he was back in school and got his Grade 12 diploma. I was so proud of him. He said he was going to college now to further his education in social work. I told him if he stayed straight I would be there for him and help him if he needed it. So needless to say I am so very proud of Rob, and I know it has been a struggle for him trying it on his own with studies and an apartment to pay for, but he knows that I'm always here to help him when needed. He now has a relationship with his son, who is also proud of him. I must say that the whole family is behind Rob and that we're all so very proud of him.

Fran

I, Shirley Connolly, am Robert Moore's biological mother and I recall the following experiences in his life.

Robert was born in the Oakville Hospital on May 29, 1972. Every night after he was no longer sleeping in a crib, I would find him on the floor behind the bedroom door. When he was two years old, I was ready to leave for work when he passed out on the living room floor. Worried, I called 911 and we were rushed to the Oakville Hospital where tubes were placed in both ears.

Roberts's father, Arnie, and I separated within a year after this incident; he left early one morning while I was sleeping with the boys and went to his mother's house, and called the police to have me removed from the house. This was after he had located his old girlfriend, Dianne, Arnie's wife today. Robert and his brother, Thomas, were raised by their father and his new girlfriend because of this.

I found in the years after he turned ten he defied authority, had problems at school and started smoking at the age of thirteen or fourteen, which I totally disagreed with. Robert became rebellious at the age of fifteen, got into a lot of trouble with the law doing break-and-enters, fighting. I also believe this is when he started using heavy drugs and drinking.

He came to reside with me off and on at the age of sixteen for a number of years. Before this time he had already met his brother, Kevin, from my second relationship, but that was when he met his other brother, Riagan.

Robert was stealing from everyone including me, large sums of money. Robert was heavily drinking and abusing drugs on a daily basis when he became involved in a relationship with Penny Bryck at the age of seventeen.

They had a baby girl, Elizabeth, in 1991 and Jeffrey the following year. During the birth of Jeffrey, Penny experienced numerous medical problems, which led to her death.

Robert started acting out even more and his daughter was taken away from him, and his son was with other family members. Robert used her death as an excuse for everything he did and all the trouble he was creating for himself with the law.

He was spending a lot of time in jail with no regard for anything his father or I had to say to him about his actions. I repeatedly insisted that he clean up his act.

In February of 2002, I went to Hamilton, Ontario, and told Robert he was leaving with me. I told him to never return there because he was causing way too much trouble. I didn't at the time know the police were looking to charge him with attempt robbery with a weapon.

This all took place two months after his brother, Arnold Daniel Thomas, was killed in a major car accident.

Robert resided with me for about two years, holding down a job without incident. After a while he started drinking and abusing drugs again, so I requested that he leave my home. Upon his leaving, he moved to Peterborough, Ontario, where he became involved with people who where associated with organized crime and who were very dangerous.

Just before his leaving and coming to reside with me yet again he landed in the hospital from being stabbed in the chest, damaging his lungs and liver, and was rushed into surgery. He had a court hearing related to this matter, which I attended with him in Peterborough.

The crown expressed its desire of wanting to sentence him to 12 years in prison for numerous charges, including aggravated assault with a weapon and breaches, but with a lack of evidence and my being present and willing to let him live with me, the judge decided he would be better off leaving their city, never to return, and living with his mother.

He went to his father's house for the summer of 2005, arriving back to my home July of 2005 happy and very excited.

Within the next two weeks he started drinking and threatening people and again stealing my bank card along with large sums of money from me, so I told him again to leave my residence for the last time.

Robert slept outside, with nowhere to live for almost seven years, going without food most of the time, freezing and having no one to turn to. Robert used to sign into the local detox to get food, shower and keep warm if only for a week at a time. Robert once again signed himself into the detox and rehab centre, which brings him to where he is in life now.

Robert has his Grade 12 diploma, along with numerous diplomas, certificates and awards, also one in his name at Georgian College. I must mention, though, he did over the years try several ways to be creative, taking art classes (he draws extremely well), locksmithing and cooking classes at Sheridan College in Oakville, Ontario.

As Robert's mother, I am very proud of him, along with

brothers Riagan and Kevin. Everyone knows Thomas would also be extremely elated with what Robert has accomplished in the last five-plus years: sober, drug- and smoke-free, does not steal from anyone and gets all the education possible in the fields he knows best, having lived this sort of life to assist others.

Shirley Connolly

Tim Connolly (biological mother's brother)

My name is Tim Connolly. I am writing this to talk about my nephew, Robert Moore. I have known Rob since the day he was born. I actually remember his mother (my sister, Shirley) wearing fuzzy slippers in the hospital when I came to visit her and walking around holding this new bundle of joy. I was only seven years old at the time but I do remember seeing Robert, holding him and playing with him while everyone told me not to drop him, Hehehe.

My memories of Robert are scattered as it was a long time ago that we were kids. I remember a birthday party at my house when Rob was very young, probably two. I think the party was for Tom (Rob's older brother). I remember running in the yard and playing with him and the balloons. It was a good day. I do remember Rob as a very outgoing and lovely child, carefree and innocent.

This period in Rob's life (childhood) is vague for me because I did not see him too much after Shirley split up with Robert's father, Arnie. I saw Rob on occasion but he was always a pleasant boy. He always, actually to this day, has called me "Uncle Tim." As Rob grew he lived with his father and I believe Arnie remarried or had a live-in girl-friend. I never knew her. Rob began getting in trouble as he was growing older. I rarely saw much of Rob during this period, as Shirley did not have custody and had remarried. Shirley did have two more boys with her new husband.

Sadly, Rob never really knew our family, especially my mother, who was a very loving woman and I'm sure if the trouble had not started she would have been closer to Rob, and Rob would have been closer to me as a result.

As a young adult, the trouble became serious for Rob and he began going to jail. I have been employed for 24 years as a prison guard and Rob began coming to the jail I worked at. I remember seeing him in the bull pin (jail cell) and him saying, "Hi Uncle Tim." I honestly was embarrassed and told him to not refer to me as "Uncle Tim," as this could cause undue hardship for him. Rob was in and out of jail, as was his brother, Tom. I was always shaking my head, thinking, "Are these boys ever gonna change?"

I also have some bad memories of Rob beating my brother (Pat) up and stealing from him. My brother would call me and say, "Rob beat me up, stole my money, smokes and booze." I remember telling Pat to stand up for himself and not to let Rob push him around. Sadly, my brother was a drunk and Rob was also physically and mentally much stronger than my brother, so he took advantage of him.

Rob later got involved in organized crime, which also landed him in and out of jail. Rob was a man now and knew how to handle himself, especially in jail. My coworkers would tell me, "You need to control your nephew. He's gonna kill somebody." This was actually traumatic and embarrassing for me and I wanted nothing to do with Rob because of his ties and criminal activity. This went on for 16 years. Rob in and out of jail, booze and drugs. I remember really not caring. Seeing Rob in jail almost became routine and coworkers would say, "Hey Tim, Robert Moore, your nephew, is back." I would respond, "No surprise there."

My mother told me about Rob's common-law girlfriend dying as a result of childbirth gone badly. I actually did feel bad for Rob, as this is very rare in this day and age. I also felt bad for the child, as it had no mother and a criminal father. Not a good start. My life moved forward and I had no dealings with Rob for a long time. I noticed he was not coming into jail as often and finally he stopped coming to jail period. I wondered what he was doing. I barely ever talked to my sister, Shirley, and was kept up to date by my sister, Mary, but she did not see Shirley either and the updates were very vague. I attended Tom's funeral (Robert's brother) on December 17, 2001. Robert was there and we talked for just a few brief moments. We exchanged pleasantries but did not really talk. Throughout my life I really never had a relationship with Rob, mainly due to three things: his lifestyle (crime); I never really saw him much growing up or as an adult; I did not trust him or his associates.

For years I did not hear from Rob or really know what he was doing. Then in 2009, a very bizarre thing happened. Rob contacted me on YouTube and asked to be friends. Rob sent me a letter telling me what he had been up to. I was shocked to read this and a little skeptical. I was not sure what to make of it. Then Rob sent me a message saying some weirdo was asking him for my telephone number and address off of YouTube. He also said this person was slandering me and out to get me.

I went through two weeks of hell, not knowing the true extent of these threats from an unknown person. They did indeed have all my info, like my address, but the phone number they had was an old one. They threatened to harass me on the Internet as well as call my house and even show up at my front door. Rob was for some reason getting emails from these people. I do not know exactly why he was chosen but it turned out to be a good thing all round. Rob put himself on the line for me. A very unselfish move on his part, not really sure why but he did this nonetheless.

It was here that I started to believe some of the things Rob had emailed to me in his original letter to me on YouTube. Rob and I talked several times on the phone while this stalker situation was unfolding. Rob kept receiving emails from this wacko and decided enough was enough. Rob (who I did not know possessed these skills) used computer skills he acquired and also a previous criminal mind to somehow track this cyber bully and potential home invader down. Rob told them, "I know who you are, so you better stop." Police in Texas were also notified by Rob, and he forwarded me a very professional letter he sent the police there. I was very impressed when not only did Rob track them down, but they were busted and shut down by him as well. Police emailed Rob or spoke on the phone, thanking him for his letter.

The situation died down and despite moments of extreme tension, it settled and everything worked out fine, thanks to Rob. I truly believe Rob has changed for the better. He is moving forward in his life and is getting himself educated and realizing there is more to life than selfish criminal activity. Things have changed between Rob and I, and I have no problem acknowledging him as my nephew and as a friend as well.

I feel strongly that big things are on the horizon for Rob. I also feel that Rob did go down enough of the wrong road in order to help those that are stuck in the negativity that life throws at them. All you have to do is remember Rob's story and believe it can happen for you as well.

God bless and keep striving high.
Uncle Tim

My biological father, Robert, was a man that I looked at as a brother because at the age of seven you don't exactly understand the difference between a brother and an uncle. I grew up calling him Uncle Rob. As a kid, I looked up to him because he was the hard case in the family. Growing up, I would have those days where he would be calling from jail on Christmas just to wish me a merry Christmas.

I guess I looked up to Rob as a brother because I called him Uncle Rob, but I only found out that he was my father at the age of 12. I sat down on the couch and when Rob was leaving after popping by one day to see how things are, I had asked my mom/aunt who my father was and she said, "If Uncle Tom has passed on and Jayson is nowhere to be seen, then who do you think your father is?" "Uncle Tom?" I said. No. "Uncle Jayson?" No. "Uncle Rob?" Yes.

Before then, I had always wondered who my parents were. I knew my mother passed on, when it came to my father I had thought he was in prison and that someday I would meet him face to face. Growing up, I didn't care to meet or get to know my father. I just wanted to go on with life and see where it took me. By the time I entered Grade 8, I noticed what my father's lifestyle was and where he was going with that type of lifestyle. I realized he was the biker type and that he was going nowhere with that lifestyle. I looked up to that, as I felt cooler then my friends to have a hard-ass for a dad, but at the same time, I couldn't be looking up to someone because of their negative lifestyle. Just like the kids that looked up to me, I told them they shouldn't look up to me for my negatives; it should be for the positive roles in life you should be looking up to. Even though my father wasn't there to raise me, I still managed to slowly follow his footsteps into the gang world. I hit Grade 9 and that's when I felt as if I knew Rob like he were my father, but even then he was still a brother. As a teen you think that wearing bandanas is cool and having a badass for a relative makes you feel cool, but you then start to realize all of it is stupidity. I never understood why I liked following Rob's lifestyle. Even though I looked up to him as a brother, I have a brother, a brother (a cousin that I was brought up with, which I call my brother) that never let me fall without having the chance to get up again and even then I chose the bandana and the homies. I had bandanas for five years until I decided to drop the act.

People wondered why and how. I feel it was because of Rob once again. He told me where my friends stood in the gang world and he told me where the gangs basically all end up. I told my brother the things I had done at school and he wasn't pleased, but at the same time he always said, "I'm glad you kicked his ass." But Rob would ask why I did it, and I always came to a blank when he asked me. When I hit Grade 10 I found out Rob was getting into counselling and I didn't care, to be honest. I was a kid and teenagers believe the world revolves around them. Before Rob had even been in counselling, my mom/aunt told me he would be on drugs, high all the time, fighting and other things he did to break the law. He would drink and fight or even around his younger years hang around Clarkson, fighting, doing nothing but getting into trouble.

I am very pleased with Rob today, and today I can call

him my dad/father. I had the honour to participate in Rob's fifth year of sobriety, as I was the one that gave my dad the medallion. This made me feel that if my dad/father can do it, so can I.

Jeffrey Moore

Michele McLeod (ex-girlfriend)

My name is Michele McLeod. Rob is my ex-boyfriend, who I met in 1992. I met Rob right after his common-law wife passed away after giving birth to his son.

Rob had a beautiful daughter, Elizabeth, who was 15 months old, who he was raising alone. My heart really went out to this man, for you could see the heartache and anguish so clear. With Rob being a young, single father, Children's Aid had an open file and was quite concerned about his situation.

I have an early childhood education diploma, which allowed me to help him and his daughter. So I had them come and move in with me to help raise Elizabeth.

Rob tried and had a hard time dealing with his loss, and responsibility wasn't easy. He dealt with his pain by drinking and fighting and eventually got involved with drugs. Eventually, Rob and I separated but remained good friends. Throughout the years Rob and I were together on and off, and then when I was with Rob, I feel that I spent just as much time alone as with him, waiting for him to get out of one of the jails.

Rob's anger and pent-up frustration got him into a lot of trouble with the law. Eventually, I had a daughter of my own and also ended up a single parent. Rob got very close to my daughter, Alexandra, and was around for holidays, birthdays and her first day of school.

As time went on, Rob proceeded to get worse with his drinking and got into trouble. A couple of years went by where I did not speak to Rob. A lot of rumours were said that he was dead or had vanished. One day Rob's Uncle Pat gave me Rob's number and said he was asking about me, which really surprised me, since I hadn't heard from Rob in years.

I called Rob and I was presently surprised that he had left town to make a fresh start. He had been sober for almost four years and was attending college, and had successfully completed a course in alcohol and addiction counselling. This was wonderful news. I always knew Rob had it in him; he just had to stop drinking. I have seen the good, the bad and the ugly from Rob and I am so proud of him for turning his life around and realizing his potential.

Congratulations, Rob, and stay on the honour roll.
Michele McLeod

I first meet Rob in Peterborough where he was living at the time. He was at a bar one night with some friends and for some reason I really took a liking to Rob, although he was an arrogant, cocky guy with a 'screw you' attitude. Rob was always very polite and respectful to me.

Rob was very unpredictable, but yet had a side to him I'm not sure many had the chance to see. I could always tell something was hurting him. I never knew what it was but seeing him so angry all the time it wasn't hard to tell that something was eating him up both inside and out.

I saw a lot of things when I was around him that I wish I never saw, nor want to see again. From drugs to constant fights and going jail, stealing and lying, I knew I was in over my head, but there was something about him I didn't want to turn my back on.

When Rob got stabbed, I had seen about enough and, like a coward in some ways, but scared in others, I turned and ran, never to look back. I regret that decision to this day, even more so when one of his old drinking buddies told me that Rob had died from a drug overdose. I was crushed, very sad and partially felt responsible. After all, I too had given up on him. That was one of the saddest days of my life.

It was about five years later when I got a message on Facebook. I literally sunk in my chair, heard my heart beating in my chest and sobbed like a baby. I couldn't believe it. To this day there are no words to explain how I felt that day.

I don't think I could tell him to his face or as part of this book how proud I am of him and how much he means to me because there just aren't enough words, but I am thankful he has been a part of my life. I think he gave doing 180 a whole new meaning and can't wait to see what he does next.

Here's to you, Rob. Go get 'em!
Kelly Doer

Robert Goundry (who I've known since I was five years old)

My name is Robert Goundry. I have known Rob Moore for 30 years in Clarkson, Mississauga. We met in grade school and became really close friends. Growing up, Rob and I were known troublemakers of Sandgate Crescent.

We would skip school a lot together with our girlfriends, but we really didn't go and do anything specific. We basically just hung out. I remember one time Rob and I were walking a friend, Tammy, home for lunch. Tammy went in and started making faces at Rob and I, so we started throwing dirt balls at her house. Rob passed me one with a rock in it, and when I threw it, it went right through the window. We both ran home for lunch and when we got back to school the police where there waiting for us to return.

Man, I really felt my heart pounding, as I was really nervous about getting in any trouble. None of this seemed to bother Rob. He just said, "Who gives a shit. It could be worse." But as frightened as I was, I knew either way we were in a lot of trouble when our parents found out. Our parents freaked out, as they had to pay for the window, but we had to make up the money through grounding and chores around the house.

I also remember Rob being allowed to spend the weekend at my house or I would go to his biological mother's (Shirley) house for the weekend in Oakville. Rob's mother was dating a police officer, who Rob didn't get along with at all. (I think it was because Rob saw him as authority figure.) So, when Shirley had her visit with Rob, her boyfriend would not come around much. We would spend the weekend up all night crank-calling people. As soon as either a woman or a man would answer the phone, we would say mom or dad, wait for a response and then proceed to say we weren't coming home that night. So, the mothers/fathers would start getting angry and demand us to get our butts home ASAP. We then started to swear and tell them no, and then hung up. I just hope their children didn't get into too much trouble over this.

In high school we would spend as much time at our girl-friends' houses or the mall as we did at school. I can't count the number of times Rob and I would be at the plaza or the ice rink and either Rob's dad or mine would catch us up to no good and grab both of us by the scruff of the neck and take us home.

When Rob turned about 14 years old, his family moved to Flesherton, Ontario, and we lost touch for a bit. We got back in touch a while later and Rob was into partying and drugs. I had met my wife and had a little girl, so I didn't have time for the parties and drugs. I cut all ties with Rob. I ran into him about two years later and he appeared to still be still using drugs and drinking alcohol, so I kept my distance once again, although I felt bad for him, but I knew I couldn't do anything to help him.

I had always said that if Rob cleaned up and stopped the drugs and drinking, I would have loved to get back in touch with him. Then, lo and behold, one day there was a friend request on Facebook and there was Rob. So I looked at his info and saw that he had cleaned his act up. So I accepted his request and we have again become good friends. We can talk to each other about anything without worrying about being judged. My wife and I are both so proud to call

Robert Moore our friend and think of him as part of our family.

We have spent time with Rob when he has come down to Mississauga to visit his son, Jeffrey, for Christmas and other holidays in the past few years. Since he has been in recovery, and I can honestly say that my wife and I have seen a big change in Rob and do wish him the best in his journey.

Robert Goundry

It is my great honour to write this for Rob Moore as he prepares to write and publish his autobiography.

In October 2003, about three months following my graduation from the Fleming College career and work counselling program, I began work as the coordinator of the John Howard Society's W.O.R.K. (Work and Occupation Reintegration Keys) program.

I greeted my first ever (professional) client, a tall, dark man, at my office door. His gruff, thick-skinned, don't-mess-with-me attitude was palpable. Following a short introduction and explanation about program benefits and responsibilities, Rob uttered his first sentences, peppered with slang and swearing, and I remember thinking, 'How will I establish trust with this man?' Though his 'biker' stature was truly daunting, I was filled with the passion to support others with a "never give up" enthusiasm. I can admit now that I was somewhat overwhelmed by the experience with this a 'hot-head' and sought support from my supervisor. Her seasoned advice set the stage for the next few challenging months of appointments. I was determined to motivate Rob to address his list of grievances and issues.

As we found common ground in a love for art, we slowly started to unravel the story of Rob's life up to his recent release from prison. An attempted-murder charge had sealed a long stint in the Canadian provincial penal system. In truth, under Rob's tough exterior lay a dormant, sweet ol' bear.

I never knew what to expect from Rob, as he often arrived smelling of alcohol or armed with a new gripe about the system, or a tale of woe that attracted more negativity to his experience on the 'outside.' His anger was never far below the surface in those early days, yet by the end of our hour together he'd leave with a bounce in his step and a wee bit of hope in his smile. Rob was a charmer and I knew when he was manipulating truth to serve his purposes, yet any small change was huge in terms of quieting his beast within. I did whatever I could to find mechanisms for a few extra dollars to lighten his world in any small way. I found pencils and drawing paper and shipped them to the Lindsay bucket when he was incarcerated for yet another infraction. We'd established a rapport that I quite honestly treasured, as he was now at least trying to take steps to turn his life around. I had planted seeds for change the best I could. I believed in Rob. The rest was up to him.

When he left the area for points west of Peterborough, we agreed to stay in touch. Off and on I would hear from him across the miles. The day he called to let me know that he had come to the end of his long struggle with the world, I couldn't believe my ears as he recited the incidents that led him to his newfound sobriety. He was attending meetings daily. He enlisted the support of his new community and a wonderful parole officer. He has become a true poster boy — lost and now found — a man of success as he ticks off his list of goals achieved.

We continue to stay in touch to this day. I am inspired by his successes and his commitment to help others. His passion continues to grow and there is no end to what Rob may achieve in the future.

I am not sure if Rob knows of the whole picture of our

time together. Some of this may come as a surprise to him. One of the ripple effects of this story is that I continue to support at-risk youth as a life coach and when I teach conflict resolution or the cycles of addiction, I tell them about this story as an opportunity to inspire them in understanding that everyone has the ability to find themselves and rise to their greatest potential as part of a decision to reach for their dreams.

Rob, may all your dreams come true!

Best always,
Janis Mansbridge
Life coach

My name is Rod Wilson, from Burlington, Ontario. I served with the Halton Regional Police Service for 37 years until my retirement in 2008. During my professional career, I had numerous contacts with Robert Moore, his brothers. Thomas and Kevin, and his uncle, Patrick Connolly.

Robert contacted me recently and asked me if I would write a few words about my relationship with him. I told him I would be happy to do so, and this is how I got to know Robert Moore.

My first assignment with the police service was in Oakville, Ontario, in 1970. This is where I first met Robert's uncle, Pat Connolly, and his mother, Shirley. Over several years I has numerous professional contacts with Pat and this led to a long-term relationship with Robert's biological mother, Shirley. Shirley was the mother to three sons that I became personally and professionally involved with. All three sons, Thomas, Robert and Kevin, had serious conflicts with the law and judicial system. Although Robert was involved in some serious criminal behaviour, he was very personable and charismatic. I took a personal interest in Robert's life because I felt that he had potential to make a good life for himself. He had to confront the demon of alcohol and drug abuse.

Between 1987 and 2005, Robert amassed a criminal profile of almost 30 convictions. These convictions included serious violent assaults, armed robbery, numerous drinking fines and breaches. He also had to deal with the sudden death of his wife after complications from giving birth and the death of his older brother, Thomas. Thomas was killed in a vehicle collision in Mississauga, Ontario, in 2001. I am sure these two losses had a profound effect on Robert and how he chose to conduct his life.

I recall taking a number of weapons (a gun and a big knife) off Robert at times, before he decided to use them and get charges that would keep him in jail for a majority of his life. I, as a police officer, did have to run the gun through and make sure it wasn't used in a major crime. Thankfully, it wasn't, as I didn't want to have to arrest him.

Robert was pretty violent with the officers I had on staff. He would fight them and give them a hard time. Most of them didn't want to deal with him because of his behaviour. One day I was sitting in my office and Robert's name came across my desk once again. I knew he was in a foul mood and I didn't want any of my staff to get hurt. So I looked to see who was on staff that day and asked two of the biggest officers working that day to come over and assist me in transporting Robert to the county jail.

I had many conversations with Robert about his chosen path. I believed that he was on the pathway to hell, prison or self-destruction. I counselled him as best I could as a police officer and a human being who was genuinely concerned about his future. I lost contact with Robert around 2005, but I did hear that he was living up north somewhere. I knew nothing of what he was doing or where he was going. I retired from the police service in 2008 and have been enjoying my time off with my daughters, my grandkids, my girlfriend, my golf clubs and travelling.

I received a call one day from a former colleague at the Ontario Police College in Aylmer, Ontario. He told me that he had a friend that was a police officer with Rama Police Service in Rama. The officer was a friend of Robert's and apparently they were doing good work with the local youth.

I was asked to call Robert. I called the number and was very pleased that we were able to reconnect. It was good to hear his voice again and he advised me that he had been clean and sober for over five years. He did not explain the epiphany that changed his life, but I am sure that will happen when I see him face to face, or I might read it in his book. He told me about his academic accomplishments and his desire to get his university degree in social work.

I am very proud of Robert's accomplishments to date and I wish him continued success in reaching his goals. I know when I talked to Robert on the phone he expressed that he wanted to open up a place to help guide the youth who are heading down the same path he was.

It is very rare, historically, for Robert to do what he is doing. It takes an enormous amount of commitment and courage. I used to tell Robert, "It is not important what happens to you in life, but what is important is how you choose to deal with it." I believe Robert finally listened to that profound advice. Continued good luck and good health, Robert. Until we meet again, I remain your friend.

Rod Wilson

Tamara, Rob's probation officer

It is an honour and a privilege to be the first one to edit this book of Rob's. I thought I knew him, but reading this has shown that our relationship only ever scratched the surface. It is evident the amount of work he has put into it.

I will never forget the first time I met Rob. I had just returned from an 18-month leave, and just getting back into the routine of seeing clients when Rob showed up for his scheduled meeting. Everyone who knows him knows he's huge and loud.

My job places me in a position of authority. But sitting across the desk from a smiling biker-type giant who was so enthusiastic about his recently discovered sobriety that he talked about it non-stop, quoting the 12 steps, quoting from the Big Book, and then questioning my understanding of what it takes to get clean, I suddenly felt inferior to his experiences. I was able to regain some ground when, to my surprise, he agreed wholeheartedly when I suggested that he had a lot to prove considering the thickness and seriousness of his criminal history.

The moment he left, I called the treatment centre. I had difficulty determining his truthfulness. I identified myself and asked if they knew Rob Moore. Of course they did, I was told. I asked only one question: "Is he for real?" I was told that he absolutely was. I've never forgotten that. It was the very first time in my career that I had met someone who was actually committed to and demonstrating significant change in their life.

In the more than five years I've known Rob, he's been nothing but real. In times of uncertainty with my other clients, I've been able to reach out to Rob for his insight into the life of an addict and asked for his help in determining someone's commitment to change. He has taught me a lot about addiction and recommended different books and videos to assist my understanding. He is an amazing, valuable resource and he is gracious enough to offer his guidance every time I ask.

In the time that I've known Rob, specifically the time he was reporting to me on probation, I was never concerned about his relapse into drugs or alcohol. On that front he was the most determined person I'd ever met. However, I regularly expressed my concern that his relapse would be in anger. For years, even sober, he was still very angry. He had a chip on his shoulder, waiting for someone to knock it off. I remember having some very frank discussions about this, having regained my footing and realized underneath his gruffness, he really was trying to improve himself.

What Rob understood when he was finally ready was that it was okay to let people know that he had a caring, empathetic side. Previously he viewed that as a weakness. I believe now he's using it to drive him towards his goals.

Rob regularly reached out to me to help calm his nerves about school. I remember how he said he hated reading, and that he had to set a schedule to get through it all. He had extreme difficulty believing me when I suggested he needed a break. I think it's true that his new addiction is school.

When he graduates, the community of Orillia should welcome the experience and knowledge that Rob will offer in the area of addictions.

For years now, I have considered Rob a colleague and his degree will only verify that. I wish him nothing but the best in his studies and I applaud his dedication to this book.

And, by the way, give yourself a pat on the back for deciding to read this book. It's worth it, maybe not now, but at some point in your life.

"I count him braver who overcomes his desires than him who conquers his enemies, for the hardest victory is over self." Aristotle

Tamara Williamson
Probation and parole officer

I'm writing this letter as a contribution to the outstanding human triumph of an individual whom I met four years ago at the Orillia Learning Centre, Robert Moore. Four years ago, as an acclaimed trustee for the City of Orillia, I was invited to speak at the Orillia Learning Centre to a class, and one of the students was Rob, who was in his graduating year, receiving his Ontario Secondary School Diploma, and he was also taking a correspondence course for addictions.

Robert, at the end of my address to the class, approached me with such enthusiasm and interest, as I had spoken about the importance of young citizens being engaged in politics and the value of a vote in our democratic society.

Robert demonstrated immediately, with a glimmer in his eyes, the determination of a young man who had, in the face of much adversity, decided to better himself and pursue education. Since that time, four years ago, Rob has graduated from the social service worker program at Georgian College, applied and been excepted in the bachelor of social work program at Lakehead University to pursue lifelong learning and a career in the field of addiction counselling and humanity studies.

It is without reservation that I commend Robert Moore for writing his biography in an effort to perhaps help so many other young people that struggle have hope and inspiration that education can provide if one is willing to set their sails in that direction.

Robert Moore has a story to tell and has touched so many people over the last few years as a motivational speaker at other learning centres in the Simcoe County District School Board.

I know his book will be a great seller!

Sincerely,
Debra Edwards,
Chairperson, SCDSB, and trustee for the City of Orillia

I first met Rob in the fall of 2005 when he came to the Seven South Street Treatment Centre here in Orillia, a residential program for men with problems of substance abuse. As part of the overall treatment program there, I facilitate an anger management course, and it was in this context that I had contact with him over the next several weeks. Upon his graduation from the program, Rob remained in Orillia because he had established a solid network of supports here for his own continuing recovery, and was in treatment with me individually through my office at the Community Mental Health Service for further professional support over the next several months.

He was tall and sturdy in stature, loud, gruff, seasoned by years of experience on the street and in the drug and criminal subcultures, and at times even a little intimidating in his overall demeanour. Six years later, he's still tall and sturdy in stature, and at times still loud and gruff, but a little more gentle and patient. He's mellowing and this is a good thing – as a direct result of his continuing sobriety, his continuing journey of self-discovery through further education and his continuing commitment to helping others whose walk parallels his own experience.

By his own admission, Rob had a 15-year history of polysubstance abuse at the point that he came to Orillia. His graduation from the program at Seven South Street was the first time he had completed a program of recovery, though he had been at another program for about two weeks at one point previously. To his credit, and as a demonstration and testament of his commitment, Rob celebrated five years of abstinence from drugs and alcohol use last fall, a remarkable achievement given his history.

Rob's accomplishments over the past several years are numerous. In addition to gaining sobriety after this history of addiction and the chaotic lifestyle that goes with it, he successfully completed his high school credits through the Learning Centre, and went on to obtain a drug and alcohol counselling diploma through correspondence (Stratford Career Institute), all of this while working on a part-time and casual basis in order to support himself. While studying at the Learning Centre he received the Lieutenant Governor's Community Volunteer Award for Students. Then, following his graduation from high school, Rob went on to Georgian Collage here in Orillia and completed the social service worker diploma and is now registered in his second year of the bachelor of social work program through university. During the time he was at Georgian College he established a bursary (Robert Moore Award) for other students, and received the Simcoe College Foundation Award.

In addition to these academic accomplishments, Rob has given back to the community in an untold number of hours of volunteer work, including the Telecare distress line, tag days for various organizations, the Lighthouse soup kitchen and men's shelter, tutoring through the Orillia and District Literacy Council. Additionally, he had been called upon to speak as a resource and motivational person at various seminars, workshops and classrooms. Rob is a strong voice for recovery through the twelve-step programs, and continues to anchor his own recovery in these principles. He is a sponsor for others whose own recovery is just beginning, and is also available to the in-patient mental health program here as a resource to individuals who might be interested in attending a self-help meeting.

Rob was nominated a couple of years ago for the Courage to Come Back Award of the Centre for Addictions and Mental Health, as an individual who has demonstrated determination in the manner in which he has persevered beyond the challenges of addiction and mental health problems to attain the goals he has set for himself.

Not surprisingly, Rob's goal is to work in the mental health and addictions sector of health care, and I believe that his personal journey, along with his continuing volunteer work and pursuit of academic qualifications, position him well in this regard. I recall with fondness a comment he made to me years ago, that one day he would have my office. It pleases me to no end that he is starting to get very close!

Brian R. Adams

Introduction

All my life I learned how to do things to try to impress others, as I believed I didn't get the attention I thought I deserved. I would act out in many ways so I wouldn't have to pay attention to my own problems and hope they would go away. When I took the plunge and wanted to be a better person, I didn't know how to properly act. I would still act selfishly, but I didn't like the way that felt. When I finally started the twelve-step program, I discovered I wanted to change from the bottom of my soul. Little did I know that this would be the hardest thing in my life to do because I had to face me, all of my emotions, and I had to put so much effort into simply looking honestly at myself.

The following pages tell of my journey, but it is not mine alone. So many others are on the road where I once was, and my wish is that by telling my story I can help put some hope back in your life and let you know you are not alone.

Chapter 1

Survival

While growing up, people saw me as someone who was loud, boisterous and a class clown. I would make noises to be noticed, muscle/bully people to get attention and also to draw attention away from others because I felt hurt and out of place and had difficulty handling it when someone else was in the spotlight.

When it came to survival in jail, it didn't take long for me to learn a different type of survival. I learned that inside I would have to do my own time, as in not butt into anyone else's business, and certainly not make noises to get noticed. To make my own time go a lot easier, I would become friends with some guys, and they were usually the guys that ran the range. They were called "servers" or "cleaners." The servers would control the TV, and they would say who stays on the range and who leaves. Most of the time those who became servers in the range were in on charges that could have them locked up for a long portion of their life. So they really had nothing to lose, as they were in for the long haul. They were the guys who would serve food to all the inmates in the range. During meal times, we used to sit out in the range, but as time went on the institution policies changed and we were made to go to our cells for a few hours to eat. The cells had a slot in the door so the servers could hand us the food.

The food that was served in the jail was regulated from the health board. They told the jail how much was sufficient to serve, but it was never enough, and I would always feel hungry. The food that I remember getting really wasn't the home-cooked meals you would get at your mom's or wife's or husband's house. This food was like eating a TV dinner, with just enough to meet the standards. So I would either get extra canteen (canteen is like a weekly store, which allows the inmates who have money in their accounts to order stuff like candy, chocolate bars, playing cards, pop, pencils and greeting cards) or we could swap some of our canteen to get an extra meal.

I was eighteen years old when I first saw the inside walls of the jails. The canteen used to be $10 or two free pouches of tobacco (daily mail tobacco), one pack of papers and two packs of matches, but, eventually, they cut back and only gave us one pouch. Then down the road they cut tobacco out in all jails altogether.

The cells were very small. At about twelve feet long and eight feet wide, they didn't contain anything other than bunk beds made for two people, a steel toilet with a sink attached to it and a mirror on the wall above the sink, which was steel but you could still see your reflection. It reminded me of looking into a steel toaster. The cells also had a bench where two people could sit and write their letters or do their homework if they were registered in school, or we would have our meals there.

Most of the time the jails would be so overcrowded that

they would put three men to a cell. Having three to a cell was a bit much; the third person had to sleep on the floor, which meant there was no room to manoeuvre to use the toilet. The toilet was an open concept. There were no doors closing you in for privacy. So when I had to go to the bathroom, I would feel ashamed knowing I had no privacy to do what I had to do.

When I was on the outside and waiting to go to court, knowing that I was going to jail, I would buy some dope, usually hash oil, or weed oil along with some rolling papers and matches or a small lighter and wrap it all up and put it in a condom or balloon. I would use Vaseline to insert it in my rectum to bring in for the guys on the range. This would allow me to gain respect with those who ran the range. And for doing so, they would give me cigarettes and supply me with extra food, and I could get protection if anyone tried to bother me.

Living on the streets requires different survival techniques. I was homeless and transient on and off for about seven years. My survival depended on where I was or what I was doing. When I wanted to get money to have a drink, I would look around for change and empty bottles to take back to the beer store, or I would hook up with a friend of mine and we would walk around with a shopping cart gathering aluminum and copper to bring to the junkyard in exchange for money. The most we could get was $100, but by that time we would be half-pissed because, while walking around, we would run into people we knew and they would offer us a beer or a shot of whatever they had.

I find it interesting that while I learned how to roll with

whatever circumstances, my higher power called my way. I grew blinders on the side of my head. (Blinders are what horses wear so they can only see straight ahead.) I was inflexible; I didn't consider anyone's perspective except my own. I would punch someone if I thought for even a second they looked at me the wrong way. I couldn't have cared less that I was going in and out of jail more frequently. Ironically, in learning how to adapt and survive in different environments, I almost self-destructed.

So which came first – the violence I perpetrated, my use of alcohol and drugs or the traumatic events that shaped my life? After so much effort into the examination of my life, you'd think I would know. It's likely a combination of all three. I do know they certainly fed off one another and the cycle seemed too hard to stop.

Chapter 2

Drugs

For a long time, I didn't enjoy the way I felt about myself, and escaping into drugs and alcohol would make all the bad feelings go away. This was difficult to do because I didn't have a job or money. If I needed a drink or a fix, it didn't matter whether someone was awake or asleep; I'd fight, steal or rob them. I remember waiting for people to pass out so I could rifle through their pockets and take their money.

When I was drinking, it didn't really matter what kind of alcohol I drank. I didn't wait for beer to get cold. Warm would do. Labatt 50, Blue, Molson OV (the OV tasted like I was drinking a class of sandpaper), Molson Canadian. Back then, all the bottles were stubby. When they became the full-size bottles, I drank cans of Crest. Crest was 10% alcohol and I only needed six to eight beers to be sloshed. Old Milwaukee bottles had about four or five beers in them, and always available at a bargain price. It didn't even have to be real alcohol; mouthwash, Chinese cooking wine (known as rice wine), Kelly's sherry wine, and sherry triple 777. I also drank homemade Portuguese wine, which used to be sold through the back door of a Portuguese butcher shop. Man, it tasted like crap, but it was better than nothing and this was very potent stuff and could do the job fast, although the hangovers that came with it were so bad and I would spend hours on end in the bathroom throwing up.

At one point, I found out that the Portuguese shop was fined for selling this wine, and that this so-called homemade Portuguese wine was made with antifreeze for cars! I freaked out and thought, "Holy. What was going through their heads? They could have killed us."

The Chinese cooking/rice wine was very cheap and very easy to get. Chinese cooking wine is basically 50-60% alcohol. I had to chase it with water because the salt content was about 20%. It was by accident that I learned it could cure hangovers. One day a friend and I had such bad hangovers, and we were panhandling to get some change so we could get some booze to at least feel better. We met a guy who was drinking clear liquid from a bottle. I asked him, "What in the hell are you drinking?" He said, "If you want to get rid of a fast hangover, go get rice wine. But just to warn you, it has an awful taste and you better make sure you get some water to drink afterwards because this will dehydrate you very fast." We thought this was a good idea, so my friend and I bought a bottle each and we walked around looking for a place to drink it. All I could think of was getting rid of my hangover and we forgot to get some water to wash it down with. We ended up going under a bridge were we would sit looking at the river. We also found an old pizza box to use as a table to roll tobacco from a few cigarette butts we picked up along the way.

I will never forget my friend's face when he took the first drink. He tilted the bottle back, took a huge swig and, when he swallowed, his whole face went white as if he had seen a ghost. After his face returned to its original colour, he looked at me and said, "Not bad. You try." Feeling brave, I said, "I eat rusty nails for breakfast, so I can handle it." I proceeded to tilt back the bottle and take my first swig. Well, I took a huge gulp and it came out faster then it went in. My friend wasn't too happy with me because I ended up throwing up all over him. Thank God it was a nice summer day and we were wearing only shorts and T-shirts. While he was freaking out on me for throwing up on him, he emptied his pockets and jumped in the river and washed off. After that he wouldn't come near me until I got at least half the bottle down and kept it down. I did manage to keep this awful-tasting wine down and my friend did come closer and sat down. I mentioned I was starting to feel pretty good, and he said he was, too. We had to drink river water to keep from turning to dust, though.

I have been told after I had breathalysers from the police or blood tests done, when I was rushed to the hospital, that I should have been dead from all the alcohol in my blood stream. That's when I started saying, "I don't have enough blood in my alcohol system."

I remember having that first drink around the age of thirteen. My brother, Thomas, and I were visiting our biological mother in Oakville, from up north, and her brother, Pat, was down visiting her, as he wanted to meet up with Tom and I. That is the first time I remember meeting him. My Uncle Pat was a tall, skinny man with dark hair that looked like it needed a combing and a messy moustache, but the one thing that stood out was his eyes. One of his eyes didn't move. It was creepy the way it stared at me when he faced me. This was because he got into a bar fight in Medicine Hat, Alberta, and lost his eye. Uncle Pat ended up getting a glass eye that did not move at all. It just looked forward. Before leaving for Peterborough, a while after my brother's death, my mother, Shirley, still grieving, informed me that two police officers in suits arrived at her home, questioning her about my whereabouts and informing her I was wanted for armed robbery. This was extremely upsetting for her, and soon after, Sergeant Rod Wilson and an officer from the SWAT team in Toronto arrived at her house, asking about my brother, Kevin, who was AWOL from jail since our brother's death.

While living on the streets in Peterborough, a few friends and I would go around on garbage night and go through people's recycling boxes, mostly the ones that belonged to the bars, and we would drink the booze in the bottom of the bottles. But we wouldn't drink right there. We would fill one bottle with all different kinds of booze. I bet I tilted about 400 bottles before I filled one small 26er, so I could sit down in the bush before going to bed and drink it. Just like a night cap.

When it came to drugs there wasn't much I didn't try. There were times I used crack cocaine on a plastic container as a puffer with tinfoil with pinholes on the top and an elastic band around it to hold it together. There were other times I got a copper pipe used for plumbing and stuck a steal coil in it, melted the crack on the end and puffed away. I would also put a fifty- to one hundred-piece of crack in a spoon, put a quarter package of vinegar that I got from a fast-food place, make sure it all melted in the spoon, then add in a part of a filter from a cigarette and use a syringe to suck it all up and bang it into whichever one of my veins I could find. I also have tried smoking heroin, but I didn't like that stuff.

I popped a lot of pills and used them in any way I could: chew them, snort them, swallow them, even bang them to get the fast high. Some of the pills I can remember using included Ecstasy, Valium, OxyContin, Ritalin, and codeine, like Tylenol 3 or 4. I remember one day I was so sick and hung over and got a great deal on 150 OxyContin pills. I actually had a job at the time, so I ate three or four of them just to hold me over until lunch time, and I went to a nearby bar and chugged a beer. I ended up taking 40 or more over the next few days. Apparently, this was a little much, because I got sick. When I went to the doctor, he told me I should stop whatever I was doing because I was throwing up my stomach liner and chunks of my liver. If I continued, I would die.

Like everyone who uses, my personality changed while I was on drugs. When I was high, I didn't seem to be very patient at all. For instance, there was a time when my brother and I were living in Peterborough in a rooming house. This house was more like a small apartment building made into a rooming house. There were about 20 different rooms that were rented and four different kitchens and bathrooms. My room was small. It was upstairs, and the room was about the same size as a jail cell (six by eight feet), for which I was only paying $375 a month. Sometimes I had a hard time paying the rent because I would borrow money or get dope on credit with my brother. My brother was selling cocaine back then, so it made it easier for me to get my dope. He lived downstairs, where his room was a lot bigger them mine (fifteen by fourteen feet). He had three big windows, which made it easier for people to get in to see him, as the doors for coming into the building were always locked.

One day I was helping my brother clean the whole downstairs because we partied all week. Everything from the bathroom, his room and the kitchen had lots of beer bottles in it. The kitchen had to be scrubbed down as someone cooked and left grease all over the stove and walls.

My brother got a call and asked me to look after things until he came back. He said he'd be about an hour or so. I agreed, and while cleaning his room, I found his stash of cocaine and decided to spark up the party. I took about $100 worth and ran upstairs to get one of the needles I had stashed in my ceiling for just the right occasion. Just before I would do any dope, I'd always get this weird feeling like I had to go the bathroom, complete with very bad cramps in the stomach, sweaty palms, and my nerves would be totally shot until I get the dope into me. I got the needle and went in to the bathroom and locked the door.

This bathroom was used by most of the people in the house, but no one else was around, so I knew I wouldn't be bothered while I was in there. The bathroom had a spoon and the filter of a cigarette already stashed from previous times, so I prepared the dope the way I liked. Normally, I would tie off my arm with anything around, sometimes with the shirt I was wearing, or a cord from the hair dryer, basically anything that would get the vein to pop. When I eased the needle in and pushed the plunger about halfway, I would begin to taste it on the end of my tongue and I instantly wanted more and would rush the rest of the needle in. The tingle would start to turn to a nice, warm, melting rush through my body. Then it would all hit. I would feel a major rush and then the "ringer" would come. A ringer is when you feel a beautiful, straight flow of a humming sound through your head. I had been chasing my very first ringer for years, but I had never come close to experiencing anything like it since.

When I first started to inject drugs, I would only need about $20 worth to get a ringer. But over years of using, this had increased in this night in Peterborough, when I needed at least $100 worth. It became more and more expensive to get a ringer.

One of the other guys living in the same boarding house (let'scall him Fred) and I would sometimes do collecting for my brother. The first couple of times we went together, Fred carried a plastic bag. It didn't take long to figure out what it was for. We knocked on a door and the people inside told us to bugger off, saying they weren't opening the door for anyone. Out of the bag, Fred pulled a plastic container filled with gasoline, which he squirted under the door and lit with a match. I remember being scared and saying there were other people to collect from and we should just move on, but Fred was determined to get the money that was owed to my brother. Within seconds, the people inside opened the door and tried to get the fire out. At the same time, Fred and I went in the house to collect the money.

The inside of the house was disgusting. Even though it was now filled with smoke from the door, I could still see pipes, tinfoil used to make crack pipes, empty beer, water and pop bottles everywhere I looked. The dishes that were lying around had fungus growing on them. We didn't want to stay long, so we got to the point about why we were there. We also told them we weren't leaving without the money or something equivalent to the money owed. The guy who owed about $250 started getting everyone to empty their pockets to see if he could come up with it. While this was going on, in a dirty mirror I happened to see a guy with a baseball bat sneaking up behind me and Fred. I moved out of the way so he couldn't see me, only Fred. I waited for him to get closer and then I grabbed him from behind, lifted him up and threw him across the room. He landed flat on his back and tried to catch his breath. I jumped on him and punched him until there was blood everywhere. I wasn't out of control, but I felt close. I looked around and said, "I have had enough. We want the money we've come to collect!" They didn't have the money. One guy was so scared he peed himself. Someone stood up and asked if we would take the watch that he robbed off someone the night before. Fred grabbed it, what little cash they came up with, and we left.

The front door was still smoking from the fire when we crossed back over the threshold, and Fred looked at me with a huge smile and said, "We just made ourselves $1,000 each and your brother will still get paid." I didn't understand what he was talking about because I didn't know one watch from the next. But Fred did, and he also knew a guy who bought watches from him to resell to people.

When we arrived at Fred's friend's shop, Fred pulled out the watch and said to his friend, "I have a really nice watch that's worth thousands." I think his friend was used to him showing up with garbage watches, because his friend said something like, "That'll be the day." Fred couldn't stop smiling as he handed the watch to his friend and the friend was clearly shocked. "Oh my God. I am going to test this watch to make sure it's all the original parts and if it is then this Special Ops Black Vulture Titanium watch is worth a lot of money."

It took about an hour or so for his friend to look over the watch and make about six phone calls, and when he finally came back to the counter, he was very happy with Fred. He said, "It's amazing you finally brought a watch I can make money on." Then he asked Fred how much he wanted for it. Fred said not less than $2,500. I thought to myself, 'This guy is right off his rocker,' because there was no way any watch was worth that kind of money. Without another word, his friend reached into his pocket and handed him all the money. I was in shock as Fred passed me $1,100 and then gave me another $250 to give me brother. I was stunned when Fred asked me if it was okay if he kept the last $50 for himself. I wasn't worried about $50 at that time.

My brother seemed amazed with what transpired and he was also happy that I had money. I had money, which meant I could have a great night smoking dope and he knew I would share with him. It seems unreal now because $1,100 could buy me some textbooks and a semester at school, but back then, that money only lasted one night. The next morning, I was back to being broke again and thinking of ways to scam more money.

Chapter 3
Criminal History

One of the toughest parts in writing this book was bringing up my criminal past with family and friends. It turns out, there's more that I've forgotten than I remembered. The memory of someone who isn't using is always better than that of someone who is. So, everyone I talked to had their own recollections.

I was with my best friend Robert G. and another person I will call Tammy from school. The three of us left school in search of lunch and we were walking and joking around, throwing mud balls at each other. We reached Tammy's place. When she went inside, she stood in front of a big pane window. Tammy was laughing, giving us the finger, so I handed Robert a mud ball that I put a rock into. It smashed a hole right through the window and it sure scared her. Robert and I ran like hell back to school.

All afternoon I waited for something to happen. Tammy told her parents and her parents called the police. The police came right to the classroom where Robert and I were, and they asked us to leave the class to face our troubles. When we got to the office, I saw both of our parents waiting for us. This is when I felt like running and not facing up to it. But I played the big shot and told Robert it was no big deal. The principal wanted to suspend us both, as she didn't like us one bit, but we didn't get suspended because the incident didn't happen on school property. The police did say we wouldn't get charged if our parents decided to pay half for the window. Our parents did agree and the grounding they gave me was worse than being arrested. At least, that's what I thought at the time.

I remember another time when I was grounded once again. There was a guy I was jealous of because he was really smart and had a girl around him all the time that I really had a thing for. The funniest thing was she never even knew I was alive. This guy was the typical "geek." He had a pair of glasses with duct tape, golf shorts with pink spandex to hold them up, and his shoes looked like black and white tennis shoes. While joking around with my friends at the side door of the school, I picked up a few small rocks and started to throw them towards this guy. No big deal, right? Well, I wasn't getting the reaction I wanted, so I threw a bunch of rocks really hard at him and broke his glasses. A teacher was outside saw me do it, so I was asked to go to the principal's office. My parents paid for them to be fixed.

Another time I was really mad at my stepmom one day, so I started a fire in the basement of our townhouse. I lit a paper towel on fire using the pilot light on the furnace, and then threw it under my dad's workbench. I ran upstairs, yelling, "I smell smoke!" Mom and dad both ran downstairs and found the paper towel burned and asked me what this was all about. I offered no reason, so I was grounded, again. Minutes later, while my parents were watching TV in the other room, I asked to make Rice Krispie squares (the only thing I knew how to cook at that time) and I was told no because I had cooked way too many of them lately. I got mad and grabbed another paper towel and turned on the gas stove, lit it and threw it in the big kitchen garbage. This time I didn't say anything. My dad smelled the burning and flew into the kitchen, grabbed the garbage pail and threw it out the sliding door to the backyard. They added to my grounding no TV, radio, phone calls or any time after school to talk to my friends. They only gave me fifteen minutes to get home and get in my bedroom. This time, I really felt the pain of loneliness and did not play with the fire again in the house.

My family and I went camping for many years at a family park called Lawson Park in Flamborough, Ontario. My family was really well liked by the owners and many other campers who went there on a regular basis. All three of us boys (me, Jayson and Thomas) didn't have to think really hard to come up with stuff to do. One day, for some reason, I decided to cut down some birch trees. Mr Lawson, the owner of the campground, caught me. He yelled at me to come to him and demanded to know what I was doing and who gave me permission to cut down the trees. The other guy I was with ran away and never did get caught, so I took all the blame. I had to work around the grounds for the whole summer for my troubles. Once again, my parents got a fine to pay Mr. Lawson.

When I was younger I would go into both my brothers' room and break their toys, just for the fun of it. I think I did it because I was paying them back for something, but who knows. I was mad all the time and created reasons to get them. Even though I always denied it, my toys were never broken, so mom and dad knew it was me. My grandmother also caught me coming out of my brothers' room and asked why I would be in there. She told my parents and it was confirmed I was the one breaking their toys.

I stole money from my parents' piggy bank. I would use a butter knife to stick in the hole and turn it upside down and get what I needed to buy a small 15-pack of cigarettes. A 15-pack of cigarettes was about $3.15 back then.

One way I dealt with my anger was fighting people, and nine out of ten times it would only lead me to be arrested and I'd end up with lots of assaults, uttering death threats, physical and verbal assaults on my criminal record.

I broke into pop machines, laundry machines and newspaper boxes to get enough money to help feed the crack addiction or so I could get some booze. One time there was a very close call because I was pulled over by the police after just having hit some machines. I had the crowbar and about $50 in loose change with me, and he questioned me for about ten minutes. He kept asking me about all the pop machines that had recently been broken into. I was sweating bullets, thinking there was no way out of this one, when he got a call and jumped into his car and took off. The adrenaline in those final moments was a different kind of high, but not the high nonetheless, so even though I was scared, I didn't stop committing crimes.

While in jail I experienced a number of lockdowns. Lockdown happens when there aren't enough guards to work the area, or inmates have acted up in an aggressive way, or when the guards smell drugs or cigarettes in the range and none of the inmates takes ownership. One time we were locked down for almost two weeks because the guards found a bullet somewhere in the jail and they figured one of us had a homemade gun. They called in the SWAT team to come into the jail and search the whole jail. The whole thing was unreal.

I was looking out the small window we had in our steel cell door and I couldn't believe my eyes. I had never seen anything like it in my time in custody. There were 20 to 25 officers all lined up to come in the range. They were all wearing a dark colour and most of them were wearing something over their faces so they couldn't be identified. Some also had shields in front of them, and then they all marched into the range. My cellmate said he had been through this a few times and told me to do whatever they asked or they would beat us. I didn't like what I was seeing and felt my heart starting to pump fast, as I didn't know what to expect, and even though I was cocky, I knew that wasn't the time to stand out.

They went to one cell at a time and made us stand in front of the cell door so they could see us. We had to strip in front of them, and once we were totally naked, they did the search like always: lift your hands, show both sides of your hand, run them through your hair, open your mouth wide, lift your tongue, move it around your mouth, then lift your privates, show underneath, turn around to show the bottom of your feet, bend over touch your feet and spread your butt cheeks, and then they asked us to put on just our underwear and back up into the slot in the door and put out our hands so we could be handcuffed.

Once handcuffed, they opened the door, yelling and demanding the whole time for us to obey them or they would force us to do what they wanted us to do. The door flew open and my heart pounded more, as I didn't know what to expect. We were escorted out the door and out of the range and told to sit in the hallway, facing the wall. We were told not to make a noise or even talk to our fellow inmates and not to even look at them for that matter. One guy decided to not obey the officers' orders and they dragged him away and the whole time I spent in the jail I never did see him again. It was my understanding that when they took him they put him in segregation, "the hole." When they did take him around the corner, all I could hear was him yelling for them to stop and it sounded like he was being shown who was boss. While we were in the hallway the police were in our cells ransacking them to find whatever they could that we weren't allowed to have. They escorted us all back to our cells and shut the door, opened the slot in the door and told us to put out hands through the door to take off the handcuffs. I have no idea if they ever found the homemade gun.

I spent a few of my sentences in the Guelph Correctional Centre (jail), which is now closed. I was in my cell reading a book when the guards came and said I had an appointment. I had no clue what it was for, as I didn't put out any requests to see anyone. I was escorted to an area they called the tower. The tower was where the big shots, like the warden, had their offices.

I was asked to sit in a room and told that someone would be with me momentarily. When the door opened, a lady came in and asked me how I was doing and if I was enjoying me stay at the jail. I replied, "Lady, I am in jail, not the YMCA. What is there to enjoy?" She didn't appreciate my humour. She was mean looking and seemed like she wouldn't take any crap from anyone. Then she got to the point she asked me if I knew why she was there, and if I knew what "red flagged" was. I answered no to both, and then my nerves started bouncing all over the place. She then said, "If someone is red flagged, it's like they are a high risk in the community, so they have to report to the police station their address and phone numbers every time they change. The reason for this is because they have repeated offences over and over and seem to be at risk in the community to reoffend. Therefore, letting the police know where they are living all the time so they can keep an eye on you." She also mentioned that this was the first step towards being classified a dangerous offender.

The dangerous-offender designation is part of the Criminal Code. The Criminal Code states it is "intended to protect all Canadians from the most dangerous violent and sexual predators in the country. Individuals convicted of these offences can be designated as a Dangerous Offender during sentencing if it is shown that there is a significantly high risk that they will commit future violent or sexual offences. The objective of protecting innocent Canadians from future harm can and will ensure in such cases that the offender will remain in prison indefinitely until that risk no longer exists. If the court finds an offender to be a dangerous offender, it shall impose a sentence of detention in a penitentiary for an indeterminate period."

Now, I was never charged with anything close to sexual assault, but I was charged with a lot of assaults, which is why I was sitting in this office talking to this lady. She asked me many questions about why I was so angry and why I had all those assaults. I did the best to answer all the questions I could without harming myself. I was really nervous and she knew it, because she kept handing me some paper towel, as I was sweating like a pig. When she had all her questions answered, she said I would be notified of the results in two weeks or so. I said. "Wow. Two weeks. Why so long? I am going to be on edge for two weeks." All she said was. "Too bad that you're so hard done by." Then she left. I was escorted back to my cell and couldn't believe what I had just gone through. I thought to myself, 'How could I let this happen to myself?'

I think it was done this way so they could watch my behaviour while I was under stress for the next two weeks. I had to watch every step I took so I wouldn't get into a fight, but still had to be the man in front of my fellow inmates. I just keep telling everyone that I wasn't myself and was coming down with the flu or something.

The day came when I received the letter in the mail. When I saw the envelope as it was being handed to me, I felt a sense of calmness come over me, as if it was all over with and whatever it said, I would accept. Mind you, if it said I was to be red flagged, I would have fallen into a deep whole trying to figure out ways to climb out, and if it said I was okay and didn't need to be red flagged, then I would be so happy, but I would try to figure out ways to not be put in that situation again.

Once the envelope was in my hand, I opened it slowly and I prayed for it to be good news and not to show that I was red flagged, as I somehow knew my life would change forever. I started to read and became happier and happier as I read on; I was given another chance to prove to that I could be a better person, though it took many years for me to actually do that.

One day a friend of mine came in with a bundle of money after he decided to rob a few variety stores in town. We celebrated his success and we called the dealer and he bought three eight balls (around $540 worth). When we ran out of money he went in the bedroom and brought out a bunch of clothing, and said, "Let's get dressed up and get ourselves some money." I was stoned and frightened, and at this time my heart felt like it had stopped, as the dope made me feel very nervous about almost everything. My friend kept asking me if I was a chicken and said if I wanted to smoke some more dope, this would be a fast way to get some money because he already took care of the video cameras. I did not like the feeling that I was having, but I agreed to go along with it. We found another guy who owned a car and my friend convinced him to be the driver.

When we all got in the car and took off, all I could think about was how much jail time I was going to get for this stupid job I was going to do. When we parked the car at the side of the building, my friend walked in the store and bought some popsicles. Once I seen that the till was open, I made sure I was covered. I put on a scarf to cover my face and an old jacket that didn't fit me at all, along with a twelve-inch blade knife, and ran into the store and demanded money, but the clerk slammed the till closed and took off running. As I was so nervous, I couldn't figure out how to open the till, so I ran out the door and got into the car. My friend was trapped inside because when the clerk took off to the back room, he pushed a button that locked the doors within a period of time. I was lucky to get out, but my friend wasn't, and he ended up getting caught buy the police. He was let go because he had a good story, but I think they did suspect him.

A week later and after many times hearing all of this on the news, I was feeling more and more nervous about going to jail, and I knew it was going to come to an end. I hid in the house and drank more and used more drugs than I normally did. During that time, my thoughts raced. It wasn't a week later I was sitting on the floor, smoking some crack and I could hear noises, like someone whispering and footsteps near the hallway door. So I said, "Shhhhhh," and then whispered (when someone on crack tries to whisper, they don't realise how loud they really are), "Someone is sneaking around the hallway." One of the girls said, "You must be pretty high if you're hearing things already." Then I thought, 'Oh my God; I must be hearing things." Unfortunately, I wasn't hearing things. I heard a huge bang and the door flew open and guns were everywhere. They asked who I was and I said I am Robert Moore. At the moment, I breathed a sigh of relief that the wait was over, but at the same time my emotions were a bit twisted because I was embarrassed to be arrested in front of my friends. So my friend and I both got arrested and taken to the Hamilton police station for questioning.

Once we got to the police station, we were strip-searched and the police looked through all of our stuff to make sure we didn't have any weapons or more drugs. Being strip-searched was degrading, even as high as I was. There's a process to it: undress slowly and pass all your clothing over, turning the socks inside out; show your hands from front and back while opening your fingers; put your hands through your hair; lift your arms and show the arm pits; lift your private parts and show underneath; turn around and show the bottom of your feet. Then they asked me to bend over and touch my feet and spread my butt cheeks. They had me dress in a blue outfit, which they provided. It consisted of one pair of boxers, one pair of socks, a towel, pants and a shirt, and a sweater.

They came and got me from the cell they had me in, took me to an interrogation room and started to ask me about the robbery at the variety store. I was told that no matter what I said, I was being charged and would be waiting to go to court, then the county bucket. They just wanted to hear my side of things. They told me they had a pretty tight case against me and my partner. They also showed me two different video statements. One was my so-called girlfriend. The other video was the guy who drove me and the other guy around to pull the robbery off. Later, I found out my girlfriend and the driver of the car had been seeing each other for few weeks and were trying to find a way to tell me or get me out of the way. Well, they got their chance. I was incarcerated for attempted robbery and sentenced to one year in jail after almost five months dead time.

I was also charged with aggravated assault from a fight

over drugs and alcohol. It was during that fight that I was stabbed with a twelve-inch blade, which lacerated my liver. I was with a friend and his girlfriend. The disagreement began like all others when you're high, about who took more than their share. But this one got out of control quickly. He and I were yelling and his girlfriend was freaking out. He pushed me and I fell, but as I was getting up I saw a knife in his hand. He shoved the knife right in my stomach. I did not see the knife go in, but I had a burning feeling when he pulled it out. I was able to stand up and I pushed him hard so I could clear the way to run out the door. I ran down the street and started to feel wheezy, like I was going to faint, as I saw blood squirting out of me.

I made it about a block and flagged down a pizza delivery guy. The guy said I could get in, but he told me not to get blood all over. So I stuffed my thumb all the way in the hole to stop blood from coming out. I couldn't feel an end to this hole and my thumb was so deep in the hole I could feel the warmth of the blood oozing out all over my clothing. I thought I was going to die. I was really weak and the driver was asking questions just to keep me awake until we got to the hospital. Once we got to the hospital, I went deeper into shock as the driver opened the passenger door and helped me out. He basically carried me into the emergency room. Once we were in, all I could see were doctors and nurses dropping everything and running towards me to help me. They rushed me into the operating room and all I could think of was the nurse cutting my clothing all off, that it was embarrassing to be stripped down in front of everyone, but it didn't last long. The doctor asked me about five or six questions and then gave me the gas and asked me to count backwards from ten.

In the recovery room, I was told I didn't wake up for about 24 hours due to the fact I was very dehydrated. I also ended up having double pneumonia, which made it hard to breathe. Never mind I had 44 staples in my chest. The recovery room was not like a typical hospital room, except for all the hospital stuff and nurses. The room was like a separate cabin that was out in the woods.

Waking up for the first time, I tried to sit up. The pain that came over me was so strong I yelled out. The nurse ran in and asked me to lie down so she could get me some pain medication. The medication they gave me was morphine mixed with Gravol. It made me feel like I wasn't even in the hospital. But it wasn't enough because I really pushed it a few days after surgery. When I asked to go out and have a smoke, the nurse said, "Mr. Moore, are you for real? You are in the hospital with 44 staples, a case of pneumonia, and when we test your breathing you can hardly push the ball in the tube!" I still wanted a cigarette, but she wouldn't let me go by myself. So I called my friend, Tommy, and he came to visit me. Tommy was one of the friends I lived with on the street. With him there, the nurse couldn't argue with me. She took off the morphine drip, but kept the tube still in my vein. I was also told not to be downstairs too long. I felt kind of wired due to the morphine, and Tommy had to wheel me down in the wheelchair, but I got my smoke.

When I lit up, I choked for about five minutes, and all I could feel was the pain, but after the first smoke I learned to take smaller puffs, as I wasn't ready to quit smoking at this time in my life. Tommy brought his duffel bag. He had two big bottles of beer with him for us to drink. We poured it in some McDonald's cups he brought so we wouldn't get caught. After we drank the beer I felt like I needed something more, though with the mixture of morphine and beer, I wasn't feeling any pain at all. I heard a phone ring, and Tommy pulled out his cellphone, answered it, and the name that he said was our drug dealer asking him if he wanted anything before he left for the night. Tommy said he was at the hospital visiting me and would call him when he left, but the dealer insisted on talking to me. When I was handed the phone, I started to feel nervous with stomach pains, the same ones I always got when I knew I was going to use.

The dealer wanted to see me, and he did while we were in the smoking area. When he arrived, he got out of his car and asked Tommy to go sit down with his driver. Really, all the dealer wanted to do was give me some cocaine. I told him I couldn't afford it, but he gave me $150 worth and said, with all I'd been through, I deserved this one on the house. When I went back in the hospital, I looked around for a needle, as I still had the plug in my vain from the morphine drip. I found a needle from somewhere in the hospital and I found a bathroom. (I was still in the wheelchair through all of this.) Once in the bathroom, I made sure the door was locked, and the wheelchair held the door shut as I poured all the cocaine into the needle and poured some water in it and shook it until it all evaporated. (This was called bake and shake.) Then I stuck it in the plug that was already in my vein. All I could notice was the taste in my mouth as it started to enter my body. I could only take half of it at the time. I started to feel the buzz and became very paranoid about getting caught. I then started to throw up, as I was mixing way too many drugs in my system. Once I stopped throwing up, the buzz stopped, so I finished off the rest of the cocaine I had left, and once again became very paranoid and started to throw up again. I think there were nurses outside asking if I was okay, because I could hear someone knocking, but I ignored it. When the buzz slowed down enough, I cleaned up and threw everything in the toilet and flushed it so I wouldn't get caught. I headed back upstairs, and when I got up there the nurse said, "Mr. Moore, where did you go? I thought you were going for one hour, not six." All I could say was, "Sorry. I was in the bathroom throwing up most of the time. I think it was from the smoking." She smirked at me and helped me get into bed. When she left and went back to talk to the other nurses, I could hear her say, "He was drinking." I fell asleep in about half an hour and for the rest of the night.

A few days later, one of the nurses who was giving me my morphine needle in the butt told me that the police were there to talk to me, but I was sleeping and they said they would come back later that week.

I started having bad dreams that night and woke up drenched in sweat and started hallucinating, as I was on a lot medication. When I began to hallucinate, I started to pull out the morphine tubing and the tubing they had for intravenous with antibiotics. I was yelling that I was getting the hell out of there before the cops got their chance to arrest me. I noticed a urinary catheter (a plastic tube known as a urinary catheter that is gently slid into the penis and is connected to the bladder) and I tried to pull it out, not knowing that it was secured with 10 cc's of sterilized water so it wouldn't fall out. I have never in my life felt pain like that. That really slowed me down from getting out of there, and allowed the nurse to give me a tranquilizer so I could sleep off all the medication I was on. Apparently, I was okay when I woke up hours later.

When the police did come and arrest me, I wasn't sure why or what I did. But they had no hesitation to let me know, and they read me my rights and told me I was under arrest for aggravated assault, and asked me if I knew why. I didn't know why, as I believe I might have had too much to drink. So I asked them why. At the same time, I started to feel like I was going to throw up. My stomach was full of knots and I was in shock from how deep I had got myself in. They told me that another individual in the house was stabbed on the upper thigh and that a butcher knife had been used, leaving the stabbing right down to the bone and eight to ten inches long. They also mentioned that after the stabbing, another person had grabbed a sewing needle and thread and sewed it up while using hard liquor to sterilize the wound. Now, I was really in shock hearing all of that.

Under the circumstances the police gave me a promise to appear and I had to report to the police station three times a week. They said if I would like to tell my side of the story, they were only a phone call away. Every time I reported, I was either stoned or drunk, and each time, the police charged me with fail to comply with probation. I ended up with thirteen breach charges.

I pleaded not guilty and when the sentencing came I was really scared and didn't have any booze or drugs to help me through it. The Crown attorney was asking for twelve years. The judge looked like he wanted to hang me. He looked like he was in a bad mood. A few hours went by and the judge asked me to stand in front of him. I was looking around to see how many police officers were in the room because I was going to run like hell to get out of there if he gave me the twelve years they were asking. I prayed so many times to just let me get this done and over with, as I couldn't handle the stress anymore. At the time, I had no idea who I was praying to.

The judge spoke in a deep voice and called my name and said that he wanted me to stand until all was read. When the Crown started to talk, he spoke very clearly as he said, "Your Honour, this is a mystery of what really went on that night." Apparently, the evidence against me was not enough to convict, so he was prepared to withdraw the aggravated assault charges if I pleaded guilty to four of his thirteen breach of probation charges. I couldn't believe what he was saying. The judge still had to decide. When the judge looked at me and asked if I would be willing to plead guilty to four breaches if he dropped the others, I wasn't stupid and I took the deal. I didn't have to go to jail at all, but I got more probation and I also got permission to leave town to live in Burlington with my biological mother. I think everyone was glad when I left Peterborough.

I met a guy in the Barrie jail and we got along great. He seemed to be well known in the jail. He gave me his number and said, "If you're ever up this way..." So, one day I called him and he came and picked me up.

We got to a place called "Hazard County." There were a bunch of people living there, and it lived up to the name. There was no hydro, no running water, no cable — nothing. But that didn't stop us from partying that whole week. While gathering up beer bottles to exchange for money, I saw half a box of bullets that were on the porch.

"Hazard County" is located out of the way, where no one is troubled by what they do there, like having bonfires or shooting off guns in the back woods. There were lots of parties with some pretty crazy people at times.

There was a woodstove going most of the time to keep the dampness out or to help us keep warm in the winter. The bathroom looked like a regular bathroom with a tub and a sink, but there wasn't a toilet. Anyone who had to poop had to poop in a portable toilet, and the toilet would have to be emptied at least once a week. We would take a shovel and make a fair-sized whole in the back woods and dump the portable toilet. If males had to pee, they just went outside somewhere.

A car battery was hooked up to a car radio with jumper cables. Speaker wires ran up the walls to hooked-up speakers all around the house, inside and out. A generator was hooked up for the use of the TV so we could watch our favourite show, which was The Beverley Hillbillies, because they were a lot like how this place was running.

We had many big fires. We would all sit around drinking, listening to music. One day, one of the guys found the box of bullets on the porch; there must have been eighteen to twenty people around. Every day, someone was pulling a trick or two on people for some good laughs. Well, this was a wild one. A really drunk guy was loaded to the gills and wasn't thinking too clearly as he grabbed the bullets off the porch and threw the whole box in the fire pit and yelled, "Run for your life! She's gonna blow!" When the bullets finally heated up, people were howling like wolves and laughing as they ran away and the bullets started to fly in all directions, even going through some cars that were nearby.

Even drunk, I knew I wanted to stay alive, so I ran like crazy to a hillside about 500 feet from the fire pit where the bullets couldn't reach me. They only went straight and not around corners. I was scared that I would get hit by one of the stray bullets. I had lots of thoughts going through my head. I couldn't wait for it to be over, but I didn't want to show my fear because I knew the type of people I was hanging with. It took about fifteen minutes before we came out of hiding, still laughing about it. The joke was the talk of the night.

Chapter 4

Summertime

Sometimes my hangovers would be so bad that I just couldn't keep anything down. The smell of anything greasy also turned my stomach. I had a hard time even moving my eyes, as they felt like I had sandpaper in the sockets. I wouldn't want to do anything but crawl in a hole and die. I knew the only way to feel better was to get a drink into me.

Once I did get the first drink into me and it stayed down, I knew I had about an hour before I would feel like crap again, so I had to make some money to keep going for the day. So, I would panhandle. People aren't very nice to pan-handlers. I would hear a lot of people judging me and some would be pretty blunt with their words and tell me to get a job. I would panhandle on Queen Street in Brampton, walk-ing from downtown Brampton, the four corners (where four different banks were located on the corners) and all the way to Highway 410. It would take me hours to go one way while hitting up almost everyone who crossed my path. As soon as I would get enough for a six-pack, I'd buy one be-cause there would have been no way I could walk that far without the six beers making me feel better.

There were a few bars that I would hang out in each week and if I stayed long enough, I'd get booze bought for me or money given to me. The problem was I would have so many lies and stories that I told to get the money or booze that I would forget what I said. So when people would ask me, I would just go along with them so I didn't look like a fool. Now that I think back on it, I probably did look like a fool; they just didn't tell me.

When Toronto had a blackout and they had to ship all their patients from the general hospital, it was a great time for me because I was just released a month prior from the hospital in Peterborough after being stabbed. My stab wound was very fresh. So, I decided to go to the Brampton hospital to look for a used bracelet that someone threw away and tape in on to make it look like I just got out of the hospital. I would tell people to get money out of them, saying, "I just got out of the hospital, but I was transferred here from Toronto general for surgery, because they lost their power but they didn't ship my belongings, like my wallet, money or my coat. So, I was wondering if you could possibly help me get the bus to Toronto so I could get my stuff." Surprisingly, I would make at least enough money for a two-four of beer and a pack or two of smokes and sometimes even enough for a room for the night.

One guy was so nice to me that he said, "It's too late tonight for you to travel while you're hurt," and he gave me enough for a room and bus money. He was really concerned about me, but I used his money to get a bootleg box of beer. This happened to me once every couple of years and, man, would I be grateful, because I knew I could use a good shower and a good night's sleep.

Chapter 5
Wintertime

I discovered that in cities, there are lots of places to sleep and keep warm in the wintertime. I can tell you that the bottoms of staircases in apartment buildings, the bushes alongside major highways, like the 401, in graveyards and snow banks aren't comfortable, and every minute spent trying to get to sleep is full of thoughts and memories of pillows, beds and blankets.

In winter, sometimes I would have to barricade myself with snow to keep warm, which is scary because if it's that cold out, you risk hypothermia. But, if you want to talk about being frightened, one time I woke up not only on the opposite side of town that I started the day partying in, but on train tracks. I had no idea how I got there. I was soaking wet, freezing, and I was seriously, painfully hung over. I reached into my pocket to see if I had any money. I didn't, and a train about ten feet away, moving towards me, started honking its horn. Okay, it was about 500 feet away, but I never in my life moved so fast while so hung over.

There were times in the winter I had to work hard to keep warm. Sometimes I would make friends with people who had tents or I would find an apartment building that had a laundry facility and I would wait for someone coming out of or going into the building so I could enter. I would find where the laundry room was and see what kind of clothing was available to steal. I would take towels, blankets, sweaters (I tried for hooded ones) and socks. I would use the socks as gloves, and I'd use towels or blankets to sleep on because the snow was cold. Sometimes the sweaters were too small, but stealers can't be choosers, and even though I could hardly move while wearing them, I knew they would still keep me warm.

People talk about how cold the winter is in Canada, but until you've spent the night outside with no coat or boots in December, worried to death that you won't wake up, don't come complaining to me.

Chapter 6

Feelings

I learned how to manipulate people in order to get what I needed, even if it was for a short period of time. Using fake accents came in handy because, for some reason, it was easier to trick people into giving me money. Knowing what lengths I would go to manipulate people also helped because I would recognize when someone tried to manipulate me. The problem was I started to think everyone was trying to pull a fast one and then I started lashing out first, before they could get me.

Anger

I was unbelievably angry at the world — everyone and everything. For most of my life, I felt the whole world owed me something. All through this book, you will see I had a short temper and didn't really care when I would throw a fit. Although I really didn't like being like that, I didn't know how else to behave. Problem was, being like that made me angrier and 'round and 'round I went, totally ignoring the fact I needed to face my true emotions and faults, get help and change!

Going around in that circle made me sad. I felt sad a lot of the time in my drinking days because all I would do was suppress my feelings so I would not have to deal with them. I tried to drink and drug them away. I would get drunk all by myself and sit listening to sad songs and cry for hours, just feeling sorry for myself. If there was a phone around, I would call most of the people for whom I had phone numbers and make up stories to talk to them and cry to them on the phone. This would drive everyone nuts.

At a really low point, I felt an overwhelming feeling of sadness. I just broke up with a lady I was seeing for a few months and didn't like the feeling of being hurt and lonely. It was my fault we broke up, as I kept lying, stealing from her and fighting with her neighbours. I was more worried that she thought of me as a drunk and a thief (which I was). I was so angry with myself that I broke up with her, which made more sense at the time. Feeling sorry for myself, I stole booze from the liquor store and headed over to my friend's house, where I could spend the night. We drank the booze and, when it was time to sleep, I noticed my friend taking some pills. I warned him about overdosing on booze and pills. He agreed if he took too many he'd likely die, but he said he knew what he was doing. When I knew he was sleeping, I got up because I was feeling even sadder about the way my life was. I was just tired of no job, no home, and most of the people I was hanging around with were tired of my lies and me stealing from them. So I wrote a note stating how sorry I was to be a big disappointment to everyone and popped a handful of the heart medication pills that my friend had.

Half an hour after I took the pills, I start to feel sick and tried to make it to the bathroom, but I threw up all over the place while running to the bathroom. I must have been in the bathroom for an hour before coming out. I used the toilet bowl on my forehead and the side of my face as something cool to keep the fever down. I knew then I wasn't going to die. I may have started to feel grateful because I don't think that deep down inside I wanted to die, but it sure would have been nice to get some sympathy and attention from others.

For days afterwards, I felt totally off balance, dizzy, and would throw up a lot. My friend allowed me to stay over a few more days or until I was feeling better. He must have known I took some of his pills, because I didn't see his pills on his dresser again while I was there, but he never did say anything to me about it.

Fear

When I was hung over or high, I would feel nervous, which would cause me to have very high anxiety, and I would fear most people and any loud noises. Most times this happened, it helped me stay safe and alive.

Fear wasn't always a very good friend of mine. I was living in Brampton, where a few others and I had a tent set up in the woods where we all lived. It was a twelve-man tent and we used some blue tarps to build a sitting area with some tables that we found in the area where people threw things out for garbage. One day, I had already been up for three days, drinking and smoking crack, and it was getting dark. All my tent-mates were out having dinner at the local soup kitchen. I decided to stay back and scrape the pipes we used for the drugs. I did get enough out of the pipes to get high, but at the same time, because I was so tired, I started to hallucinate. I saw people with flashlights and heard dogs barking. So, naturally, I thought the police were coming for one of my buddies for robbing a bank or something. I ran about 100 feet into the woods and covered myself with brush that was lying around so no one could see me. I have no idea how long I was there. My friends didn't even see me as they walked by. I could hear them talking to each other, asking where I was. They had an eight ball of crack they wanted to share. I thought they were the police pretending to be my friends to lure me out. My fear was at the highest level it had ever been. I could still see the flashlights of the "police." My friends left about three hours later and it must have been four hours before I could muster up enough nerve to get up. I walked away from the tent. I didn't go back to the tent for days. I decided to go to the detox centre for the week to refresh my thoughts. Detox didn't last long.

Numbness

I got so used to being on drugs and getting stoned as a way of dealing with my emotions that I became numb to how I was supposed to feel. And if I felt something I didn't like, I'd cover it up, because stoned was the only feeling that felt good. In doing this, I became emotionless towards people. I could not empathize with anyone and really didn't care about anyone at all. I felt like I hated everyone I met, which made me isolate myself for a long period of time. The only time I wanted to be around people was when they had booze or dope, or I had a stash that I could get into to come out of the morning blues. If I wasn't around people, they couldn't judge me and I wouldn't see them judge me and feel bad about myself. At least, that was the idea.

Impulsive

Impulsive means having a tendency to act on sudden urges or desires. There were many (too many!) times I would act impulsively and later regret it. The fighting, showing my anger and hurting someone's feelings for no reason felt good. It was like bringing them down to my level, where I hurt all the time and felt nothing but hatred and anger.

Many criminals who act impulsively often end up in jail cells because of the need to feel good, and a hatred of the world. Of course, I'd be too hung over or high to know why I was in jail, but lots of times I didn't really care.

Jail isn't the only place I've ended up on impulse. I remember being in Cambridge, Ontario, and telling the girl I was in love with that I was going to go to the store for smokes. I went to the bar instead. I had just enough money to get one or two drafts. Somehow I ended up partying with a bunch of people I didn't know, but I must have liked it because I woke up about a week later in Peterborough, which is about 220 kilometres from Cambridge. Being impulsive also means being irresponsible and hurting people you love.

I had no idea what happened during those seven days. All I knew was the girlfriend was going to be really pissed off, as I was only going to the store for smokes. When I started to think of how I had hurt this woman for whom I was starting to have some really deep feelings, I would just end up intoxicated because I did not want to face my own problems. I ended up staying in Peterborough for almost five years, drinking, drugging and going in and out of jails. It wasn't until I was one year sober that I finally called her, just to let her know I was okay and that I was sorry. But when I called, she said she had been really pissed off with me for the longest time. She called the police station, hospitals and any friends who knew me. Then she told me she wasn't ready to stop drinking and smoking marijuana and that she was happy I called so she could stop worrying about me.

I later found out, while I was in the treatment centre working on my emotions and problems, using a twelve-step program, that I ran from her because I was starting to fall in love and felt scared of commitment. I was scared of commitment because I was so hurt by the death of Penny that I became frightened of falling in love because I was scared I would lose someone again. Today, years later, I feel I am starting to open up and let others in.

Aggression

There was a time four people (two couples) and I were drinking all day in the bush. We had put our money together and got three two-fours of beer to enjoy on the nice, warm, sunny day.

We all sat drinking, joking around, playing cards on a table we made out of cardboard that we found behind the grocery store and used beer boxes for the legs. As the day went on, we drank the first case of beer within a few hours. Before we started the second case, we all decided to put the rest of our money together to get tobacco and rolling papers and something to eat. One of the other guys (who I will call Jason) and I walked to the store, got what we wanted and ordered an extra-large pizza. While we walked out of the store, the police asked to speak to us. We knew we didn't do anything wrong, but we were well known to them and they enjoyed harassing us.

When I asked why we were stopped and questioned, one officer said they were interested in the way we lived and couldn't believe we hadn't died or been in jail for a long, long time. The other officer said he just had to show us who was the boss. It was about a half-hour before the police finally let us go and said, "We are watching you."

Jason and I got the pizza and headed back to the place in the bush where we were partying. Upon arrival, Jason's girlfriend was sitting by herself and we asked where the others were. "They are having sex in the bush just over there," she said. So, we all joked around more and ate some pizza.

The others finally joined us again. They ate some pizza and drank more beer. It was starting to get dark, so we decided that we should all gather some wood to start a fire. (We were deep enough in the bush that no one would see the fire.) We planned to stay the night there.

The next morning, before everyone woke up, I was hung over and we only had a about three beers left, so I drank them really fast before anyone got up and I lay back down, waiting for everyone else to get up. When they all woke up, they were bitching about how awful they felt. So two of us gathered up all the empties and took them back to the Beer Store while the rest of them started to panhandle so we could get another case of beer to help make us all feel better.

Once we got the case of beer, we went back to the bush again. As we all started to feel better, Jason and the other guy started to play fight. They both asked me to join them and play fight, but I said no because it always turned into a real fight. The other guy would not let it go and called me names, like "wimp" and "chicken shit." I didn't like being called names and my anger started to rise. It was always high, so when someone pushed the right buttons, it didn't take me long to lose it. I drank a few beers really fast, trying to ignore him, but he kept shooting his mouth off and then asked me how I could have made it in jail all the those times unless I was someone's bitch.

I did try to hold back from fighting him. I called him a lot of names, too. I started to walk away, but he threw a beer bottle at me and called me a "goof." That's one of those words you never call anyone who's done any time in jail. The burning feeling all over my chest exploded and when I got close enough to him I turned around really fast in a half-circle and struck him as hard as I could. When my fist connected, I felt his jaw break and saw a few teeth fly out of his mouth. The worst part was that the impact of the hit made his whole body turn really fast and he broke his lower leg bone. He dropped like a stone and started scream-ing. I took off when I heard the ambulance sirens. Some-one in the parking lot saw what happened and called 911. I found out later that his head hit the cement on the ground and he had blood coming out of his ears, which meant he had to have emergency surgery to drain the internal bleeding in his brain.

The next day, I went to a place where the homeless people went for lunch. It was something like a soup kitchen, but it was just a nice lady who owned a house and liked to help out. The lady of the house called me over to tell me I wasn't allowed to walk on the premises again, as she thought I was too much trouble. I asked her what she was talking about and she said, "The police were here with a picture of you, looking to charge you for manslaughter if the guy you hurt died." I only briefly felt bad, because he had it coming and totally deserved it. At the same time, I felt proud of myself that all the people in the house were looking at me like I was a badass. Problem was, I liked that feeling.

The next day I found out the guy seemed to be strong enough to make it through surgery, but he was still in the hospital after a few days. His girlfriend went to see him, and he asked her to make some phone calls to see if they could get a place to live in Oshawa (their hometown) because when he was discharged from the hospital, he just wanted to go and not look back. I also heard that he told the police he had been through enough, was scared for his life and didn't want to press any charges.

Before I stopped drinking, I would get upset pretty easily and would punch the drywall or kick things, not caring about how much damage I was causing until I calmed down. Then I would try to figure out ways to fix the drywall. This knowledge helped me to become a contractor later in life. While attending a twelve-step program and going to a treatment centre, I learned that I had to be stripped of my emotions and built back up one by one so I could identify them and react appropriately because, when I drank, I was a time bomb and showed a lot of aggression and attitude towards people if I didn't feel my own needs were being met.

Didn't understand my emotions

While I was drinking and drugging, I would use to cover up the way I felt. I let the alcohol and drugs rob me of my emotions because I couldn't identify my emotions or tell how I was feeling, except for the anger I felt. When I did get sober and clean from all the substances I was using, I felt that I honestly didn't understand how to feel. I did not know what to say to anyone who talked to me because I allowed myself to become angry and have a closed mind to what others would say. Therefore, I didn't understand how to feel. It wasn't until about three months into the Seven South Street Treatment Centre program that I started to really notice a change in my feelings for other people.

Chapter 7

Tragedy

Cousin Tim's death – June 28, 1991

My cousin, Tim, lived in Mississauga. Tim was like a big teddy bear. He was a weightlifter and worked at the powerhouse gym, but, man, was he well liked for his kindness. At the age of 22, Tim was returning home after visiting his grandparents in Guelph, when he lost control of his car and was thrown from the vehicle after it veered into the west lanes on Highway 401 and collided head-on with another vehicle near Guelph Line in Burlington.

I was incarcerated at the time Tim died. I remember being in lockdown for three days. Lockdown is where the unit in the jail is not allowed out of their cells except for an hour a day for yard, shower and a fast phone call.

I phoned my aunt and before anyone could answer the phone, I felt a weird feeling come over me like I was hit so hard that the wind was knocked out of me. My Uncle Dan answered the phone and told me about what happened and said my aunt wasn't in any shape to be talking right now, which I respected. After all, she has just lost her son.

Tim and I were pretty close. Every summer, Tom, Jayson and I would stay at my Aunt Fran's house, but the rule was that we had two weeks to get a job or we were to go back up north, where the nearest store would take you about a half-hour to walk.

Tim had a lot of connections with people, as he lived and worked different jobs in the area for years. One day, Tim asked us if we wanted to work in a warehouse in Toronto. He talked to a friend and said we could have an interview right away. Tom decided to get a job in a pizza place instead, while Jayson and I took Tim's offer. We worked there all summer and returned up north for the winter for school.

I have to laugh while I tell you what happened. Tim and I used to go out and visit people late at night, but my Aunt Fran (Tim's mom) wouldn't allow it, as we needed proper sleep for work. One night, Tim and I decided we were going out no matter what. We tried to go downstairs to see if she was sleeping or in the kitchen so we could sneak out. But she was wide awake, so we went back upstairs to try to figure out another way. Now, my Aunt Fran wasn't a mean person. In fact, she would give you the shirt off her back to keep you warm. We just didn't want to get in any trouble. We just wanted to go out and hang out with friends of Tim's.

Tim and I came up with a really good idea: go out the window and shimmy down the aluminum soffit/downspout. This was a two-storey building. If one of us fell, we would be looking at a fifty-foot drop, not to mention what we would break after landing. Tim and I didn't hesitate to climb it, not thinking of any consequences. I went first, after we pulled out the screen, by putting one leg out, then the other while holding on the window frame so I wouldn't fall. Once I got a good grip on the downspout, I let go of the window sill. I started to feel nervous, so I tried to go as fast as I could without hurting myself or falling. When I got about halfway down, Tim started to climb out and shimmy down the downspout. I had to move fast because it seemed like Tim had done this once or twice before.

When I reached the ground, I was feeling relieved and thought, 'What if I fell? How bad would I hurt myself if I did fall?' Tim was almost down and I heard someone behind us yelling out, "What are you guys thinking? You could have fallen and really hurt yourselves." I looked over saw my Aunt Fran with a smirk on her face, saying, "How were you guys going to get back in the house without me knowing?" Tim reached the ground and started to laugh really hard, saying, "Busted." This made me laugh, too, and we ended up going back in the house where Aunt Fran lectured us for about half an hour. Tim looked over at me as I said, "Wow. How were we going to get back in the house?" Tim laughed again and said, "I didn't think that far. I just wanted to go out and see my friends."

Another time Tim went out with friends and watched a hockey game. They were all drinking, which was okay with my aunt because Tim didn't drink and was always back home in a respectful time. While Tim decided to have a few beers this night, he must have drunk six to eight beers and was sloshed. When it was time for everyone to leave, two of Tim's friends decided they would try to carry him home. Tim was six-foot-two and 260 pounds. He was massive. He worked out all the time. When my Aunt Fran opened the door, she saw two smaller guys under both of Tim's arms. It was as funny as anything I'd ever seen, but this was neither the time nor place to laugh. Tim needed guidance up the stairs to his room, where he could sleep it off.

My Aunt Fran got me and Tim one day as we were trying to sleep in. She came downstairs and told us it was time to get our butts up and ready for work. We asked for another five minutes and she said, "If you're not up in five minutes, I will pour a tub of cold water on you." We laughed, thinking it was a joke. My aunt came downstairs again to make sure we were up, but we were still sleeping. She got a big bucket of cold water and poured it on us. I learned then that whatever Aunt Fran said she'd do, she'd do. I never did sleep in again in the summer months.

While I was in jail when Tim died, I heard there were more than 100 people at his funeral. At times, I would go to Tim's grave site after I went to probation meetings, as it was just around the corner. I would go there beforehand and stash a big bottle of beer, which was equivalent to four or five beers. When I left the probation office, I would walk down the street to drink the big beer. Sometimes I couldn't get the beer into me fast enough.

Uncle Rick's death – November 28, 1991

I didn't really know my Uncle Rick, as he was divorced from my aunt on my biological mother's side, but I did know that Rick was having some problems seeing his daughter. So, he hanged himself one night after drinking a twelve-pack of beer in one of the houses he was building. I met Rick about a year before his death.

Rick and his girlfriend, Tammy, and I did some partying together before he died. We smoked marijuana and, not as often, crack, and ate some mushrooms, but we mostly drank together.

Tammy's death

Tammy, Rick's girlfriend, went right off the deep end after Rick's death. Tammy got mixed up in a lot of cocaine, drinking and whatever else that was offered. Tammy was a lot like me. She had a hard time facing her own problems, so she would hide and cover them up with some dope or booze.

I believe that all the long nights of drinking, drugging and no sleep got the best of Tammy. One night, when she was out partying with her friends, she seemed to think that she was on the first floor in an apartment building because, as I was told, Tammy and some friends were talking about some stuff and Tammy said, "Wait. I will show you. I have it in my car." She then walked out to the balcony and climbed over the railing to go to her car. But Tammy was on the seventh floor. When she fell, she landed beside a bush and was still able to talk. When her friends ran downstairs to go see if she was okay, all they could see was blood and could tell she was in pain. One of her friends said that when she stood over her and asked if she was okay, Tammy said, "I guess I fucked up my life this time." Tammy ended up dying that night.

Common-law wife, Penny Ann Bryck, July 5, 1967 - July 20, 1992

Penny and I met in Burlington. We both lived in the same apartment building. Penny lived on the sixth floor with her father, Russell, and sister, and I was living on the twelfth floor with my biological mother. Penny was four years older than I was, but I always acted older than my age and also looked older.

I saw Penny for the first time while she was in the swimming area at the apartment building, which I could see from my balcony. I asked questions to people I knew around the complex to find out if she was seeing someone, or who she was.

To my advantage, my brothers, Kevin and Riagan, were friends with her sister. I was very shy about meeting her, so I made sure that I had booze the day I met her. Penny did have a boyfriend, but I kept asking her to come to parties with me.

I think she came because I hung around all the people who would cause problems for others in the area. We were all called the "Warwick Court troublemakers." Every night, there would be fights in the catwalk and people being robbed. There was never a shortage of booze.

One of my friends, Dave, had a barrel of booze he was making. When it was ready, he invited me, Penny and a bunch of our close friends to come over to play cards, watch the football game (I never really enjoyed watching sports; I just liked the booze that went with it) and we would all drink this swish he made and get right ripped.

Finally, I asked Penny to leave her boyfriend and be with me. She said no at first, but Penny liked the attention she was getting when she hung around me. Penny and I became really good friends. I felt that I loved her from the very first day I saw her.

Penny got pregnant with our first baby and asked me if I would straighten out my lifestyle so we could raise the baby right. I agreed, but that meant I had to turn myself in to the Barrie police station to deal with some charges. I did eventually turn myself in and spend some time in the Barrie bucket, and Penny waited for me to be released so she could be with me again. When Penny had our first child, Elizabeth, on May 12, 1991, I was unfortunately not able to be there because I was incarcerated.

When Penny got pregnant with our second child, I did slow down my drinking a lot and tried to work like any regular family man. My work history was scattered, due to the fact I wouldn't show up because I was too hung over or still drunk from partying all night. So I ended up on welfare with Penny and my daughter, Elizabeth.

Penny didn't have any problems throughout her pregnancy, except for me stressing her out. The day Jeffrey was born, I thought I would get up and make a nice breakfast for the love of my life. I got up around 6 a.m. before Elizabeth would wake up. She was now nine months old and would sleep until around 6:30 or 6:45 a.m. I made bacon and eggs just the way she liked them. Eggs over easy, and she loved her bacon strips to be crispy. She liked brown toast with butter. So, I put all this together with some orange juice and put it on a TV tray, along with a red rose.

When I went to wake Penny up to surprise her with breakfast in bed, she looked up at me with her still-tired eyes and said, "I love this part of you. I just wish you would show it more often." Penny asked me to take the food out to the table and she would join me before Elizabeth woke up.

Penny went to the bathroom and came out holding her stomach and said, "There's something wrong. I'm spotting blood." I asked her to sit down on the couch and wait five minutes to see if she was okay. Minutes later, she started to bleed more heavily and told me to run to the nearest pay-phone and get an ambulance because she needed to go to the hospital.

We didn't have a phone because we couldn't afford one. I left to call the ambulance and while they were on their way I asked for my youngest brother, Kevin, to babysit Elizabeth while we were at the hospital.

Penny was taken to the Burlington hospital. She asked if she could be taken to the Oakville hospital so her family doctor could deliver the baby, but Penny was dilated too much. Contractions were too close and that they didn't want to take the chance because they were worried at the fact she was still bleeding. Penny had been four to six centimetres dilated and her water still hadn't broken.

Penny would talk to me while she lay there and we talked about our future plans. She mentioned that the drinking would have to stop, as she was getting sick of my mood swings and not being able to afford things for the kids. She said if anything was to happen to her, she needed me to be strong for our children, but I just blew it off with "Don't worry. You're going to be okay," and I told her I loved her.

Every time Penny would dilate or feel a contraction, she would grip my hand so hard it hurt. Around four in the afternoon, the doctor came into the room and told us he decided to give Penny an epidural (the most popular means of pain relief during labour) and asked me to leave the room while he did this. When I came back in the room, Penny said the doctor had given her a needle about a foot long and it hurt like hell. All I could say was, "Babe, they know what they are doing." It didn't make her feel any better.

At about 4:15 p.m., in came the doctor to break her water, as Penny was dilating more and her contractions were seconds apart. Penny then yelled out that she had to go to the bathroom before she shit the bed. The doctor said this was a natural feeling before you give birth. The doctor then asked Penny to start her taking deep and long breaths and to push really hard. When she took her second breath, I could see the baby's head slowly come out. Penny was holding my hand pretty tightly and yelling at me, "You're never going to touch me again!" and "Rob, I am going to make you feel the pain I feel right now." I was called almost every name known to man and I believe she made up a few new ones as we went on.

I had never seen childbirth before, so I felt very overwhelmed and definitely in shock as this life we had made together came out of Penny. When I saw the baby's head start to show, the baby looked to be off colour, a bit purple. Penny continued to yell profanities at me as the doctor tried to get her to take one more breath and then push. It was a few deep breaths and pushes later when the baby finally came out. They had to cut the cord, and then the nurses rushed the baby to another little table. They announced we had a boy and that he had all five fingers and toes. At the same time, they got the baby to breathe. Once I heard the baby cry, I had tears in my eyes. I was so happy. I looked at the clock and saw it was 4:35 p.m.

The doctor then had to get Penny to push out the after-birth, but it seemed that this was a major turnaround in my, the baby's and Penny's life, as I felt Penny's hand tighten up around my hand. When I looked at her, she started experiencing an epileptic seizure (a sudden occurrence of signs or symptoms that are the result of an abnormal activity of the brain). Penny started to convulse and her eyes rolled. I knew then there was a big problem. I yelled out, "What the hell is going on?" Then I could hear "code blue" and a bunch of nurses and doctors ran in. One nurse took the baby out and another came and walked me out to another room and said someone would come and see me in a bit. "Code blue" refers to a cardiopulmonary arrest at many hospitals. This doesn't necessarily mean the same in all hospitals.

The room was about seven feet long and seven feet wide. It had a few blue loveseats and a small end table, which had a phone on it. The walls were a calm, pale colour. I sat in the room wondering, worried and clueless to what was going on until about a quarter to six, when a nurse came in the room and handed me Penny's jewellery and wallet. I asked her what was going on and all she said was, "Would you like to see a Father?" I had no idea what she was talking about and said no. I didn't know at the time she was asking me if I wanted to see a father from a church. Ten minutes went by and the doctor finally came in and said, "I hate this part of the job. Do her parents live close by? If so, you might want to call them, as they might be here for her, too." The doctor made sure I was okay before he left and I immediately got on the phone and called Penny's father, Russell. Russell and I never did see eye to eye from the beginning. When Russell got there, I met him outside and walked him to the room I was sitting in to wait for the doctor to come in and let us know what was going on.

When the doctor came back in, he said, "Now that I have both of you here, I want you to know that Penny has had serious complications and is now in a coma, and she has a 1% chance of making it through, and both of you have to make the decision of letting Penny live on life support or pulling the plug. Either way, I need you both to sign the paper of what you agree on." Russell asked if we could see her. When the doctor left the room, Russell and I discussed for a few minutes what we should do and we both decided that because she would never come out of the coma, why let her suffer? We signed the papers to let her go.

This made me feel very hurt, empty and lost. Penny was the love of my life and I didn't want to lose her. As Russell and I sat there looking at Penny and all the dried-up blood that was around Penny's orifices from when she had haemorrhaged, I was speechless and just wanted to hold her and never let her go, but I knew they were only giving us a few minutes to see her. Russell and I signed the paperwork, and when we left all he would say to me was that my daughter, Elizabeth, would be fine, she's at his house with his wife and kids until I got back on my feet.

If Penny were still alive today, I would have married her without a thought, and I would have made the best out of raising our children together. See, I had this vision that I would grow old with her and we'd be able to raise our children together. Man, I loved Penny so much.

Grandmother Jean's death, November 14, 1993

My grandmother was the mother of my father, Arnie Moore, and my Aunt Fran. My grandmother died in her 66th year. I called her Nanny when growing up.

Nanny was a real bitch when she wanted to be. I'd seen her pick sides with those she liked and those that she didn't like. One day, there were children around the age of ten to twelve and they threw an egg at her house, hitting her window, on Devil's Night. You wouldn't have known she was in her 50s when she grabbed the corn broom and ran like crazy to chase the children. She did somehow catch one of them and made him a warm bucket of water with soap in it with a cloth so he could clean the mess they left on her window.

I used to get suckered into playing poker with her, or other games, all for money. She loved money, and she loved winning, so playing with her was never fun. Nanny was very competitive and didn't like to lose. So I would save all my pennies and play card games with her day in and day out, not knowing how to get out of it, as I didn't want to hurt her feelings. The only thing was I couldn't figure out was how to save up enough pennies to play her. Then I got smart. I finally realized she won all the time because she would change the rules as she went on. So I started stealing pennies off her without her knowing it. This way I could afford to play her and she never knew she wasn't getting ahead at all.

Brother Thomas's death, December 17, 2001

Thomas Moore, my brother, died in his 30th year in a car crash that happened on Dundas Street in Mississauga.

I was living in Hamilton at the time. It was December 17, 2001, and I had the TV on, but without sound. We had the news channel on for Toronto and I saw a car crash in Mississauga, where I used to live. I was pretty high at the time and remember thinking, 'Wow. Some family was going to have a crappy Christmas,' not knowing it was my older brother that had been killed.

A day or two later, I was at my house with a few others getting high. (The place I was living in was a known crack house in town.) There was a loud knock on the door, which sounded like the police, so we scattered to get everything cleaned up while one of the girls yelled out, "Be right with you. Just hold on." That was the first time we had the door open in a few days, as we'd just been smoking dope the whole time. When we opened the door, there were two undercover police officers standing in the hallway, and they stepped back as all the smoke in the apartment flew out. They introduced themselves and asked to speak to Robert Moore. When I heard that, I yelled out, "Shut the fuckin' door and lock it!" I was in a panic and thought they were there to arrest me. But the police were faster than the girl. They stuck their foot out to keep the door from closing and said that they weren't there to arrest me, that they needed to tell me there was a death in the family.

When the police told me I would have to call my Aunt Fran because my family was trying to get a hold of me to tell me about a death, I immediately thought something happened to my parents while away on vacation, or to one of my children. I immediately started to feel angry, overwhelmed and depressed, all at the same time.

The police stayed there until I made the phone call to make sure I was okay. While I was so nervous to find out who died, I lit up a smoke and one of the officers asked one of the others in the house to open some windows to let the place air out, as it smelled really bad. My Aunt Fran answered the phone when I called and told me I was hard to find. I didn't know what to think. I was freaked out and needed to do another blast to relax, but the police were still there. My aunt finally told me that it was my brother, Thomas, who died in a car crash. She said my father had flown in from Florida, where he was on vacation, and that he would come to pick me up and bring me to her house to attend the funeral. I told her where to find me so dad could pick me up the following day.

I was in total shock to find out about my brother's death, and when I hung up the phone, the police asked if I needed anything and said if I did, they would help me. Well, what I needed was a huge blast of crack. I knew they wouldn't help me out with that and I just wanted them to leave so I could have one. I told them I was with friends and would be okay. So they left.

When they left, we closed the windows up again and I didn't wait for them to leave the parking lot before I got the pipe out and put some ashes on it, then put a really big piece of crack on the pipe, lit the lighter and puffed away. When I inhaled all the smoke, I could feel a rush of calmness come over my body. I felt like I had no more problems. In reality, that feeling only lasted for about fifteen minutes.

My dad came to pick me up. I was still awake (for the fourth day in a row) after partying or smoking my problems away. Anyone who had dope that night was getting me high because they felt sorry about what happened to my brother and knew I was going to the funeral the next day. My dad wasn't too impressed with how I looked and told me I looked like crap. He asked me what I was doing for the last few days. I just ignored him. He knew what I had been doing.

When we got to my Aunt Fran's house, it was about eleven o'clock in the morning. I grabbed a beer out of the fridge, but when my Aunt Fran saw me she said, "Oh my God, Robert. You need to sleep that shit off." She told me it was my last beer today. She then told me to go clean up. So, I drank the beer, went to have a shower, crawled in bed and slept until ten o'clock the next morning without waking up.

My parents bought me some appropriate clothing for the funeral and my Aunt Fran cut my hair. I was really looking rough, as couldn't remember the last time I had a haircut.

When the funeral was over, my dad drove me back to Hamilton and I could see that he wanted to tell me I should move out and get my butt in to get some help, but he never said anything. I felt like a huge disappointment to him, to my family and to my brother, Thomas, as though maybe he shouldn't have been the brother who died.

Grandfather Arnold's death, January 21, 2008

My grandfather, Arnold, was the husband of my Nanny and the parents of Arnie Moore (my dad) and my Aunt Fran, but he wasn't the biological father of them. I never knew my biological grandfather. Grandpa was French-Canadian and when he got mad at me, my cousin, Tim, or one of the brothers, he would speak in French, which he knew no one would understand. My grandpa died in his 74th year from Alzheimer's disease.

I remember seeing Grandpa while he was in a nursing home in Mississauga. He did not recognize me at all, so he asked me who I was, and when I told him my name was Robert Moore, he got up and walked over to his dresser, grabbed his wallet and walked back over to me with a huge smile from ear to ear. He said, "Look at this." It was his birth certificate. I said, "Yes. That's your birth certificate." He said, "Look again. We both have the same last name."

One time, he went to my dad's house in Flesherton to spend some time away from the city. It was a typical winter and there was about four to six feet of snow. Grandpa decided to get out of bed at about six in the morning and grab his suitcase and walk out of the house and down the street. He didn't even take the time to put shoes on. He just stayed in his socks. When my dad woke up and looked around, he wasn't sure where to find his father. When he went outside to look around, he saw his shoes still there, but footprints were leaving the house and going west. Dad decided to drive and follow the steps, as it was -30 C. My grandfather was found in no time at all, up around the corner, lying down with a cardboard box covering him.

My dad went up to him and asked him to get in the car and go home to keep warm because he'd catch something, and my grandpa yelled at him to get away. Grandpa insisted that my dad was with the mafia. My dad was a fairly stocky man with a big beard. His car was all white, and Grandpa though it was a mafia car. The only way he would get into a car was when my dad called the police, and they drove him home.

My grandpa was really happy when he got to see his wife, Jean (my Nanny). On one of the days when Nanny came to visit him, my grandpa decided to push her around in the wheelchair and introduce her to all the people he knew. No one realized until later that she died right there in the wheelchair. My grandpa told people she was just sleeping.

The difference in Grandpa's death and all of the others in my life is that when Grandpa died, I was sober. I actually felt what it was like to grieve the loss of someone I loved. With that came all of the grief for the others who died before their time. I'm proud of myself for not turning back to drugs and alcohol and numbing myself to the pain of grief. And you know what? I made it! I got through my pain and I feel great. I'm still sad at having lost those good people, but I can now remember the good times and smile.

Chapter 8

Family

Elizabeth

My daughter, Elizabeth, was born in May 1991. When she was born, I was still incarcerated for minor charges. Upon release from the Barrie bucket, I moved in with Penny and tried to be there as a father, a boyfriend, a partner, a true friend. Still, not wanting to give up the booze and some of the friends I was hanging with kept me in the dog house with Penny.

Elizabeth was fifteen months old when her mother died and Penny's father, Russell, stepped in and took her in to live with him for a while. When I found another place and moved in with a lady, Michele, we decided to have Elizabeth move in with us. I was still drinking heavily and had some pretty bad hangovers at the time.

Elizabeth would sleep in a blue moveable bed that could be packed in a bag for transferring when needed. It was a travel crib. The crib was about two feet long and three feet wide (approved by the Halton Children's Aid Society). Elizabeth had not yet mastered how to climb in or out of it, but she did have a great set of lungs on her to let me know she wanted to be changed or out of the crib.

I woke up around 7 a.m. one morning and I couldn't

hear Elizabeth, which seemed odd, as she would always be up and yelling for daddy around six to six-thirty. I just thought she was sleeping in late. Michele was still sleeping, as she was never a morning person. So, I just stayed lying down, enjoying the peace. Then I smelled something that did not smell right. At first I thought someone farted, but there was much more to the smell. Elizabeth had ripped off her diaper and started finger-painting on the walls with her poop. She had it smeared from head to toe and all over the walls, wherever she could reach. I ran the bath while throwing up at the same time because I was so hung over.

While Elizabeth was in the bath, I was trying to get all the crap off her and ran some clean water with bubbles. I turned the TV on and had a few cold beers to try to fix my thoughts so I could be there for my daughter.

I used to take Elizabeth to the park and to my parents' house so they all could see each other. I was able to spend a lot of time with her, as I decided to stop working and tried to raise her on welfare (Ontario Works). They called this father's allowance, and I would receive a baby bonus. Both would still be very tough to live off of, but I still found a way to drink and smoke cigarettes.

When Russell and his wife (the mother of a few of his children) did not returned Elizabeth one weekend, I decided to call him. He said he wasn't going to return her to my house because he thought I was a bad influence on her, and he took me to court for custody.

Russell did get custody and I was to see Elizabeth only at the Halton Children's Aid Society in Burlington. I had to find my own way to and from the office. While living in

Burlington without a driver's licence and not making much money for the bus, I found it hard to get there. I asked friends with cars to drive me at times or I borrowed a ten-speed mountain bike to ride back and forth, until I bought one for myself. This ride would take me about two hours each way.

There were times I rode the bike all the way there before I could find out Russell had cancelled the appointment. One time I rode in close to my daughter's birthday. I went out and bought some gifts and wrapped then up nicely for her to open. It looked like it was going to rain, but I took the chance anyway. I had asked all my friends who drove (there were only about four or five) to drive me, but they were all busy. So, I decided to take a ride on the bike. I put Elizabeth's presents in a garbage bag and stuffed them in my coat, which was hard to do because the one present was bulky, but I did the best I could. I was starting to feel tired as I rode along Lakeshore Road, but all I could think of was seeing my lovely daughter's face as she opened up her presents. I got more than halfway and it started to rain ever so slightly.

When I got closer it started to rain even more. It poured down and I was starting to feel exhausted from riding in the rain. When I finally got there, I started to smile. I found a spot to lock up the bike. I looked around and didn't see Russell's car and suddenly felt a bad feeling come over me. I started to get really worried, so I walked into the building. The lady behind the desk looked at me and she didn't have the usual warm smile. So, right then and there, I knew something was up. When I approached the desk, soaking wet, she said the worker would be right out to see me, which was a normal part of the routine. The only part that wasn't was the fact Russell wasn't sitting there with my daughter. When the worker came out, she asked if I needed a towel to dry off and couldn't believe I rode that entire way in the rain with gifts in my jacket. Then she broke the news that I knew was going to hurt: Russell wasn't feeling well, so he cancelled the appointment. I sunk in my chair and started to cry. I couldn't believe Russell would be so selfish, and I was also thinking of the long ride home in the rain. Luckily, the worker was getting of work and offered me a ride home because she saw the pain I was feeling.

Russell had a habit of not showing up, and I wouldn't find out until I physically got there. When we went back to court, I told my lawyer it was too hard on me to go two hours each way to see my daughter when Russell only lived four blocks away from me, and I asked if there could be a different way to see my daughter. The judge agreed to let me see my daughter through a third party. Otherwise, I was allowed to see my daughter with Russell, as long as there was an approved person there to supervise the visit. Russell had never been okay with any of the people I chose to have there. I asked if my Aunt Fran, my dad and stepmom could be there, and all he kept saying was, "Rob, it's over. We don't have to let you see her again unless it's at the Children's Aid office." I called Children's Aid and they said they couldn't do anything because my case was closed.

I would send mail to Elizabeth for her birthday, Christmas, and send other stuff for holidays, but all my mail would be returned and my daughter would not receive them.

I knew I had the right address because it was the address Russell gave to the courts and it was on all my paperwork. This became a normal thing. I also tried to phone many times to talk to her, but Russell or his wife would tell me she wasn't there and they made up many excuses for me not to see her. Sometimes I would phone while I was drinking and Russell would get mad at me and tell me to not call while drinking. That night, I must have said a few choice words to Russell on the phone and I ended up with the police at my door, arresting me for threatening Russell.

I didn't talk to or see my daughter for years, until one day I wrote her on Facebook and tried to make things right between us. Elizabeth wrote back and we talked for a bit on MSN, but she kept saying that she was hurt from what I did and that she didn't know who to believe about the truth. Therefore, she really didn't talk to me much, maybe once every six months when I saw her sign onto MSN. I did get to see her and spend time with her for the first time in 18 years as I dropped out of college and moved to Brampton with my high school sweetheart. (This only lasted eight months or so.) She and Elizabeth got along really well. She set it up that Elizabeth could come down for the weekend and spend time with us.

I didn't know how to react to first seeing my daughter who I missed for all those years. When I first got up in the morning, I was feeling sweaty and overwhelmed (very excited) to be able to see my daughter for the first time in many years. I felt like a kid in a new toy store. When I did get to meet her, I didn't know how to react. I wanted her to like me. My first thoughts when I saw her were, 'Wow. She is beautiful,' and 'Looks a lot like her mother.' Elizabeth gave me a hug because I gave her one. Elizabeth's grip was not very strong, which gave me the impression she was very nervous also. That weekend we talked a lot, but I slowed down when I saw her get uptight with me when I was trying to explain what had happened in my life that kept me from seeing her. I respected her and changed the topic.

The high school sweetheart I was living with had her own daughter from a previous marriage. She was eight years old and got along really well with Elizabeth, so they spent a lot of time doing things together while I just watched and enjoyed the fact that I had my baby girl there. When the weekend ended, I called one of my friends I knew in the twelve-step recovery program, who came over to drive her to the train station, where she would get the train to go back to Burlington. That's where she was living with her Russell.

Elizabeth was twenty minutes early to catch the train, so I stayed with her. As we waited, Elizabeth and I talked about how the weekend went for her and me. She told me she was very nervous and didn't know what to say to me, as she really didn't know me. I looked down on the ground and saw a tiny, flashy thing, which turned out to be a necklace turtle pendant. I asked Elizabeth if it was hers and she said no, so I offered it to her she said, "No, it's okay. You keep it to have a memory of this day." I did, and to this day I still have it put away to keep for that memory.

I felt a very lonely feeling come over me when she got on the train and waved bye. She emailed me to let me know she made it home okay. It was the last time I saw her face to face, but I have talked to her on Facebook, MSN or email a few times. She is unsure of what to say or think of me because she has heard so many different stories that she doesn't know who to believe. I just keep hoping one day she will want to spend some more time to get to know me as a father.

Jeffrey

My son, Jeffrey, was born July 20, 1992, a few minutes before Penny had her complications.

When Jeffrey was born, I wasn't allowed to take him out of the hospital due to the circumstances. The social worker refused to let me bring him home because of my drinking and emotional state after Penny had died. So, my Aunt Fran took Jeffrey home with her and I am ever so grateful because I couldn't imagine where he would be today if no one in my family had helped out.

My Aunt Fran was working and running her own day-care through agencies in the area. I remember her having a lot of patience, as she would babysit five children, all different ages. As he got older, Jeffrey would come home early from school or would have a day off and he would help Aunt Fran with all the children. This is how he became so caring for children.

As time went on, I continued to get into trouble with the law. Jeffrey would hear about it because my Aunt Fran would tell him (so he wouldn't end up doing the same things and end up doing time himself).

I never wanted to call him while I was in jail or when I was drunk because I never wanted him to turn out like that, but on holidays like Christmas and Thanksgiving and on Jeffrey's birthday, I would try my best to call him just to stay in touch. If I happened to be in jail during one of those special holidays, I would call him from jail to talk to him, but I didn't want him to know why I was in jail. I just wanted to get him to realize I cared for him and his sister, Elizabeth.

I called many times while I was drinking, and my Aunt Fran would lecture me about her rule. Her rule was that if I wanted to talk to Jeffrey, I wasn't to call while I was drinking. One night, I decided I didn't want to hear what she had to say, and I said, "I called to talk to Jeffrey, not you." My Aunt Fran wasn't the type of person you could just tell what to do. She was pretty firm with her choices. Later that week, I called again, sober this time, and my Aunt Fran asked me if I was finished with my foolishness. I didn't know what she meant, so I asked her. She told me I had been very rude on the phone and that I threatened to kick her door in. Man, was I embarrassed to hear how I acted, but I just added it to the list of me acting stupid and once again I decided to go get drunk with friends and try to forget it.

Jeffrey and I have been pretty close for most of his life. I would come down and spend time with him, which I was only allowed to do when I wasn't drinking. I really tried in my own way to get to know him for who he was. When I finally sobered up for good, he spent some time in shock. It took a few years before I could prove to him I was telling the truth about staying sober and cleaning up my act.

There have been many talks that Jeffrey and I had to

have to let him know the road I went down wasn't the road he should try. Jeffrey used to hang with the wrong crowed, and I blame myself, as he often heard while he was growing up that his "uncle Rob" was in trouble with the law or he'd hear about people I was hanging with. Jeffrey was suspended many times from school for fighting because he let his anger get the best of him. Like a lot of kids, I think he thought my life was "cool." So I guess he saw me as someone to look up to and started to follow my path.

Jeffrey made a big turnaround in the summer of 2009 and shocked me, my aunt, uncle, cousin, his friends and his school. Right out of the blue, Jeffrey decided to ask my Aunt Fran to take him shopping to get new clothing. She just thought he wanted to get a new pair of pants or sweater, but to her surprise he wanted dress shirts, ties, dress pants, shoes, coat, etc. Jeffrey and my aunt spent $2,000 on new clothing, but it was worth it, as Jeffrey wore the clothes to school the next term and when going out. When just hanging with friends, he would wear jeans and a T-shirt.

The best part of Jeffrey making this turnaround was he slowly started to change his friends. The way he was now dressed didn't really suit the people he was hanging around with. Jeffrey had a change of attitude and it was hard to believe, but even his teachers would ask my Aunt Fran if this was the same Jeffrey.

Jeffrey has always made me proud to be his father. But when he handed me my five-year medallion, I experienced a feeling I will never forget. When Jeffrey was standing up talking from his heart, I couldn't believe that this was my son speaking, so grown up and dressed extremely nicely, with a nice pink dress top and a matching tie. He sounded so sincere and professional, almost like he was born to speak in front of crowds. When Jeffrey passed me the medallion, I was almost in tears over the fact he agreed to hand it to me.

Jeffrey still to this day is living with my Aunt Fran, who raised him. He has graduated high school and landed himself a great job. Today, Jeffrey is proud of me and this makes me happy. I didn't get clean and sober simply for the sake of being reunited with my children, but I do find it one of the great rewards of it.

Uncle Pat

Like I mentioned earlier, I met my Uncle Pat when I was thirteen years old. He was the one who gave me my first drink and possibly my first beer. He was a very hard worker and loved to be alone. Pat worked at Hamilton Builders Supply in Burlington, bagging sand (25 cents a bag) and when I hung around my Uncle Pat, I would work with him so we could earn some beer money. I enjoyed his company and it became a way to get out of my house. We would hide about seventy-five to 100 empty bags in the sand or across the road so we could get free money to drink. After a while, the boss would come outside and walk across the road and get all the bags, bring them back and would tell us we wouldn't get paid anything until we got all of the bags done, and he would have someone watch us so we couldn't hide them anymore.

Pat was a dirty kind of guy with the "I don't give a crap" attitude, but at the same time he was well liked through the community. Pat had a long moustache that always looked like it needed to be trimmed, something many suggested he do, but he liked it too much. His clothing was often smaller than he was, and his pants made him look like he was waiting for a flood. In other words, they were a few inches shorter than they should have been.

Pat was living on the streets for about ten years and had a dog named Rusty, which was well trained, and you could tell he loved him very much. Pat lived in the bush near downtown Burlington, where he would have access to everything he needed, like a beer store and a grocery store where he could buy chicken or pork chops to cook over an open fire. Pat would use a grill from an old stove to cook on. The variety store was also located close by, so he was able to get his smokes. His lifestyle for some reason drew me to it, and I started hanging out with him more and more and drinking excessively and I stayed with him at times, sleeping on top of cardboard, and a blanket that looked like it could use a wash.

Pat did end up with a few apartments, but I think he forgot that he didn't have a maid because his place was never clean unless he was sober for a good week. He would hibernate when he went through his hangovers. Unless he knew someone was coming over with booze, he wouldn't even answer the door.

Pat loved his animals, although he wouldn't clean up after them, but he would always make sure they had food no matter what. I remember seeing Pat take back empties to the beer store just to get cat food because the dog or dogs would eat human food. Pat had a very small place that was way too small to house the two dogs and seven to ten cats he had, but he loved the location.

Pat loved to drink and he also had a mouth on him. He would speak his mind whether you liked it or not, which landed him in many fights. One day when I was walking to No Frills on Brant Street, I saw the police leaning over someone and asking if they were okay. It was my Uncle Pat. He was so hammered he couldn't even make it home, so he just lay down on someone's front lawn and went to sleep with his dog lying beside him. The police got him in the car and took him home instead of arresting him because they knew he was harmless, as they'd been through this a hundred times.

Pat was a huge hockey nut; he loved the Toronto Maple Leafs and wouldn't miss a game unless passed out cold or in jail. Pat had three TVs in his small bachelor apartment. There was an old floor-model TV on the floor, and on top of it he had two twenty-one-inch TVs. Each was on a different hockey station, but he would have only one turned up loud (everybody thought he was deaf) so he could hear it and nothing else. Pat would holler and scream at the TV, telling them to pass it, call the penalties, saying, "Offside!" One night, Pat and I were at his house for the playoffs and we bought a box of twenty-four beers each for the game. The Toronto Maple Leafs were doing well and if they won this particular game they would have moved on to the finals. I laughed as Pat yelled at the TV, like always, telling the player not to hog the puck and to pass it. He got so pissed off because one of the players didn't pass and tried to shoot it at the goalie. He yelled out, "You missed because you're not a team player. If you would have passed like I said you would have gotten that goal!" He threw the beer bottle at the TV. The beer bottle shattered the TV screen, leaving us with nothing because Pat was a nice guy and had given the one twenty-one-inch TV to his neighbour, who didn't have one, and the other he sold for a case of beer.

Back in the day, Pat was a pretty good fighter. He didn't care how big or tough you were. He could stand his own and he won a lot of fights. Pat had a mouth on him, but as time went on and he became older and he couldn't back it up with a fight, though he would try very hard. When he would shoot his mouth off when I was with him, he would start it and I would be the one to step in and fight the guy. I hated to fight, but I was so angry with how I felt all the time inside myself I would just jump right in and do it.

I saw my Uncle Pat really wasted many times. He could drink at least thirty beers and smoke a lot of marijuana at one time, but this time he had been going strong for about two weeks straight. He finally had enough and wanted to go home with a beer in his hand. He left, but unfortunately didn't make it home that night. It took about thirty days before he got there. Pat was so drunk he thought the police car that was sitting outside of the variety store was a cab. So, he jumped in the back seat and when he shut the door behind him he locked himself in. The police officer came out of the store and noticed a man sitting in the back seat drinking a beer and smoking a cigarette.

Pat was on probation for some other stupid stuff he did while drinking, so the officer decided to arrest him for breach of probation to help him dry out. When Pat finally called me and let me know what he did, I laughed so hard I was crying. When Pat was released twenty-one days later, he looked great. He was clean, he had shaved, and even trimmed his rough-looking moustache. But all this lasted about a week, and he went back at it again.

Now, I admit I wasn't the best nephew Pat could have had, as I would rob, fight, steal from Pat as I became greedy with my alcoholism. I knew he couldn't do anything to me and I guess I took advantage of this.

Although I stopped drinking and carrying on, my Uncle Pat remains doing all the same stuff, drinking. He did slow down, as he has a hard time breathing. He did quit smoking, but not his drinking.

Chapter 9

12-step Program

I met a lot of people in while in a treatment centre. I never thought treatment could work for me, but it really gave me a new way of thinking that helped guide me through the hard times. In the five years I've been sober, I have had several sponsors take me through the steps and I have learned so much from each of them.

Today, I can also say I have friends who will be there for me without wanting anything in return. I have total respect for the people who I have talked to as a friend or as a sponsor through the twelve steps so I could became a better man while in the community. Believe me; while going through some of the steps, I bawled my eyes out, and I am talking snot flying and all. All they could say to me was, "Is that it? You have held all of that down for so many years." I thought it was too hard to deal with, which is why I tried hard to keep the feelings away with drugs and booze.

I had many friends while I was growing up. I used to hang with all walks of life, including people who loved and were caring to organized-crime figures. It's weird, but everyone I came into contact with has been influential on my behaviour. I'm just glad I had some positive influences in my life, or I don't think I'd be where I am now.

I quit smoking December 26, 2006, and I'm still not smoking. When I quit smoking, I thought it was the worst ever. It was even worse than quitting drinking and drugging. I tried to quit smoking so many times and just couldn't do it, but this time it has been so different.

One day I went home from school, as I was upgrading to achieve my Grade 12 diploma. When I got home, I was just itching for a cigarette and I knew I had a half-pack of smokes hidden just in case, so I grabbed one, stuck it in my mouth, and with my other hand I would grab it back out. It was like my one hand was the good and the other one was the bad. This happened a few times before I finally grabbed a small garbage pail I had lying around and broke the cigarettes up in small pieces so I couldn't smoke them.

I looked around and found some rolling papers. I was going to take the tobacco out of the garbage pail, roll it up and smoke it so I could stop this stage, where it felt so unbearable. I could not believe I was so addicted to cigarettes that I could felt like this. I then ripped up the rolling papers and poured a tea I had from hours earlier. That way I wouldn't want to smoke it.

I was in tears. Wanting a cigarette so badly, I rolled up in a ball on my bed and cried like a baby. That's when I decided to pray, not knowing how or to whom, but I did say, "If there is a higher power of some sort, this would be the time to help me through what I need to make it as a non-smoker." I fell asleep and when I awoke drenched in sweat, the bed was soaked like I'd peed, but it was all from sweating. Although I felt at ease, something happened that I couldn't explain. I sat up, looked around and did not want to have a smoke at all. The urge left for a few days. This was amazing. I had never thought I could make it through, but I realize that I did not make it on my own because before I had the nap, I prayed for help.

Today, I still pray, but now I pray in the morning. Every morning, I roll off my bed and go on my knees and I and ask for guidance to make it through the day. I pray for help so I don't become the monster I was before while drinking. I pray that I don't smoke, drink or do any drugs just for the day. Every night, no matter what, I pray just to say thank you for helping through the day and hoping that I didn't have to make amends to anyone that I hurt throughout the day.

I have no idea who or what I pray to, but the feeling it gives me is what I like about it. It's almost like I am being guided by awareness of my emotions, because all through my recovery and still ongoing, I have definitely been facing my own emotions. Step four of the twelve steps gets you to look deep inside yourself, to make a searching and fear-less moral inventory of yourself, and step five says we must be entirely honest with somebody if we expect to live long or happily in this world.

Once I did steps four and five, I felt a huge weight lifted off my back, and when I went home I went over all five steps just to see if I missed anything or was not willing to talk about something. I was convinced that I was telling myself the truth. As time went on, I ended up doing three different fourths. Each helped me reveal different stuff that was hiding in my subconscious mind. It might have been buried for about twenty years before coming out.

All the way through, and including time in custody, I sketched. It relaxed me. At one point I was on Ontario Works and tried opening my own business. I was going to make big money, but it fell through.

Drawing used to take me to another place where I didn't have to worry about stuff. I expressed myself through drawings. Too bad I didn't listen to them. I only drew when I felt like it. What I should have done was draw when I didn't feel like it, like when I wanted a drink or another hit or was asked to go to do a job.

The twelve steps guided me through what I needed to go through in order to save my life. Without going through them, I'd either be classified as a dangerous offender (which would mean I'd hurt someone really badly) or I'd be dead.

Chapter 10

Education

Schools I went to:

Elmcrest Public School (Grades 1-6)
Hillside Senior Public School (Grades 6-8)
West Credit Secondary School (Grade 9 and part of Grade 10)
Grey Highlands Secondary School (Grade 10)
Adult Learning Centre (The rest if Grade 10 to Grade 12 graduation, 2007)
Stratford Career Institute, Drug and Alcohol Counselling (diploma, 2007)
Georgian College, Social Service Worker (diploma, 2010)

At age thirty-three, I made a choice to go back to school at the Adult Learning Centre and I got my high school diploma. I remember the first time I went to the Learning Centre for class. I was very nervous. I didn't know anyone to hang around with to make it easier for myself, so I sat at the back of the class. I was new to Orillia. I didn't know anyone, and I was more than ten years older than most of my classmates. So I just sat there looking around at all the people laughing and having a good time. It took a while, but I realized there were a few who where my age or older, which made the situation easier to be a part of.

The first few months I found it hard to focus because I was just three months out of a treatment centre and I was about six months clean and sober. I was still learning how to cope with everyday life problems without using any substances. The problem was a lot of the students were young and did a lot of talking about alcohol and pot.

I started showing my anger in the classroom and was asked to go home a few times for the day to cool off. I had to sit in a separate office at times to do my work because I was bothering others in the class. I started seeing an anger management counsellor so I could learn how to deal with things differently. I was seeing him for a few years while going through the Learning Centre.

I was still letting other people affect me. For example, it would bother me big time if someone was typing on the computer right next to me and I was trying to focus on my homework, or if some of the people in class would have a conversation not meant for class but instead a bush party.

My anger management counsellor had to come to the school one day because they were fed up with my attitude. I had to sit in a meeting with the principal, vice-principal, anger management counsellor and teacher. Man, did I feel awkward sitting there with mixed emotions, hearing how I would either overreact or exaggerate the truth.

The teacher had a lot of hope for me. I am not too sure why, but it seemed that she believed in second chances and she must have seen something the others and I couldn't see. The others might have been too afraid to spend extra time on me, thinking it would have been a waste of time. Keep in mind that I was practically daring people to kick me out of school. That way, I would have had an excuse not to complete my diploma and I'd have had lots of people to blame.

During the meeting, I was asked to sit in the hallway for five or so minutes so they could talk amongst themselves and make their decision on what they should do with me. While in the hallway, I had a hard time sitting still because I was so nervous and felt I should just walk out the door and say to hell with it, but I knew every time I felt like this I would run and use drugs or booze to cope. So I didn't run, but I did close my eyes without taking a second to think if anyone was looking at me and I prayed to whomever would listen to me and I said, "If there is a God, help me make it through the way I feel, and let me identify how I feel."

I stayed in the hallway and waited for them to call me back into the room. They had all decided I could stay if I would sign an agreement to continue to see the anger management counsellor on a regular basis, and I wrote a one-page letter to the vice-principal, saying why I thought it was important for me to be given the second chance. It turns out the principal and vice-principal wanted me to leave for a year and come back after I dealt with my issues of anger and sobriety.

After I found out I was staying and walked out of that room, I really felt overwhelmed because I thought everyone had given up on me a long time ago. I was so happy that I was given the chance to make things right. I tried hard to do what was necessary to make it through to the next term.

No matter how much something bothered me, I did the best I could to show everyone I wanted to have my education, and that I deserved to be there.

My homeroom changed the next day to the classroom of the teacher who stood up for me, which really benefited me in the long run because I was very weak in my English classes. This teacher had majored in English, so I felt great about the decision that was made because I finally had seen that someone believed in me when I even had doubts about myself. This made me feel I could do it. After all, I only had a year and a half until I graduated with my Grade 12 diploma.

Every day, some of the students in class would brag about how high or drunk they got the night before or how they just couldn't wait for break time to smoke a joint. Just hearing that would make my stomach feel upset and make me think of my old war stories. (War stories are when people brag or talk highly about so-called good times they had while they were drinking and drugging.) So, when I felt like I was either getting upset or thinking too much about booze or drugs, I would journal how I felt, or call someone — a sponsor.

I slowly learned to ignore how others acted in class and really started to focus on my future. And when I started to get some really nice marks on my assignments, which made me feel good about what I was doing, I decided to go up the community college and see what they had to offer. I made an appointment to see a career counsellor.

Also, when I was going to the Adult Learning Centre, I took a correspondence course for drug and alcohol counselling from the Stratford Career Institute, located out of Toronto. I received a diploma December 7, 2007, and passed the class, being 1% away from the highest honours. When meeting with the career counsellor for the first time ever, I thought about getting a university degree in addictions, but I would have needed a recognized college diploma first. (They did not recognize the correspondence course I did for addictions because Stratford was a private college that wasn't known in the area.)

I was then told there was a new program starting in September, the social service worker program. I could get into if I got all my credits and passed everything I needed to get my Ontario Secondary School Diploma. I already invested one year in the Adult Learning Centre and completed a majority of the credits I needed. I was starting to feel overwhelmed about achieving a goal that I wanted to do for so long but couldn't because I was kept hostage by the insanity of the booze and drugs.

I didn't realize how fast the end would sneak up on me, as I was just focusing on trying to get my homework done. Surprisingly, I was doing well and the marks were rewarding enough for me to keep wanting to achieve this goal.

I applied in the course at Georgian College and I was accepted. I would never have thought that I would have been able to get my Grade 12 diploma, never mind get accepted into a college program.

Through the years, I heard people talking about their experiences in college and they would talk about how hard it was, but most would talk a lot about the parties they had in their dorms. Even I knew of the parties because, when I was about sixteen, I hung around some guys who would go to some college in Toronto to parties on the weekends, and I would tag along.

Back then, walking into a college dormitory, all you could see was a very long hallway with everyone's doors open, a big cloud of smoke lingering over head, a lot of people drinking, laughing and having a great time. Everyone was nicely dressed — the men with their blue jeans and nice dress shirts, and the women wearing skirts with nice blouses. Even the people who were just wearing their jogging suits didn't stand out as much as me. I was easily noticeable wearing my Ozzy Osbourne "Bark at the Moon" T-shirt, which was torn from a previous fight. One time, I had a bright blue cast from breaking my arm after falling off a roof while on a jobsite in Brampton, while drunk. The thing is, I wasn't working there. I just wanted to steal the copper for money.

Knowing what I knew from past experiences from parties at colleges and universities, and what people were saying about how hard the work was and the high expectations, I was very scared of being in college. But I was honest about it and talked to one of the counsellors about how I felt. She assured me that was not the way college was. She offered kind advice and encouragement and gave me more confidence to stay in college.

I was told I could also take a course in the summer to lighten the amount of work I had to do. When September came and I became a full-time student, I would have less to do and it would be less of a struggle to complete. The course I had to take was college communications, which helped me to know how to write an essay at college standards and learn how to apply rules of the American Psychological Association citations and sources book that was used in the college.

The Georgian College Barrie campus is where I had to commit to going every Wednesday for a three-hour class (between five and eight o'clock at night). I did commit to this as I was still going to the Adult Learning Centre, but it worked out okay because the hours at the Learning Centre were from 9 a.m. to 1:30 p.m. I would walk the half-hour home from the Learning Centre just to have enough time to change, eat and grab my bus ticket to get on the Greyhound. I had to be on the 2:35 p.m. bus so I would arrive in Barrie at 3:15 p.m. or I would be late. So I rushed to get on that bus.

I would do the majority of my reading that I had to do that day on the forty-minute bus ride there, because all week I didn't have any time with the homework from the Learning Centre and the correspondence course I was taking. One day when I was on the bus going to Barrie, a drunken guy thought he recognized me and called me David. I thought it was funny because he keep saying things like, "Hey, David. Remember the guy that you and I beat up? Well, he broke into a store in Orangeville and he could hear the cops coming so he decided to just run and go through the big pane glass window and the funniest thing happened. While he was going through the window, he slammed into a telephone pole and knocked himself out." Or, while at the back of the bus, he would open another beer and would start to laugh and ask me why I was reading. "Are you trying to be smart?" I didn't see that drunken guy on the bus again after that night.

Once the bus arrived in Barrie, I had to catch a city bus, which took another forty-five minutes to get to the college. I usually got to class at about 4:30 p.m., just a half-hour shy of class starting. What a pain! But I kept reminding myself that this was all worth it.

Sometimes class would finish early, around 6:30 p.m., and I felt upset because I had to wait until the bus would arrive at 8:30 p.m. I decided I would sit outside and read more of a textbook I had for class and watch all the other college students and talk to them about their courses. One student really put a scare into me. He told me he was having a hard time keeping up seven classes because there was way too much homework. He was in his second year in the electrical engineering technician—power course. The moment he told me this I had serious doubts of being able to make it through college. So, the next day, I made an appointment with the same career counsellor to consider alternative ways of making it through. When I met up with her, she told me to focus on one term at a time and not put my thoughts into the next term or I would get myself overwhelmed.

There were many times I called people while feeling overwhelmed and asked for help or just vented. A few times I was so upset and called my old probation officer, who was really good in English. She got me to calm down and then asked me to come in so she could help me with the essay that I was frustrated with. It was a relief to know I had so much help as long as I was willing to ask for it.

Upon passing and completing that summer course, at the same time completing my high school diploma, and just a few months away from completing my correspondence course for drug and alcohol counselling, I was really starting to like learning, but I was still nervous about the course load, thinking I'd fried my brain with all the drugs and alcohol, or I didn't think my brain would allow me to remember all the stuff I needed for college because of all the fights I was in. I did not think I was good enough in English to be able to pass. Despite how I felt, I entered full-time in the social service worker program at Georgian College, with the guidance of the college counsellor.

I couldn't understand why I was getting migraines. The migraines would start slowly and then come on strong. They felt like someone was literally stabbing a sewing needle through me eye. This would only happen on my right side. The doctor told me they were "cluster headaches." As the name suggests, the cluster headache exhibits a clustering of painful attacks over a period of many weeks. The cluster headache peaks in about five minutes and may last for an hour. Someone with a cluster headache may get several headaches a day for weeks at a time — perhaps months — usually interrupted by a pain-free period of variable length. The doctor then proceeded to tell me it was caused by stress. So he procribed me blood thinners and gave me a note that he wanted me to take to the school to give to my counsellor. At that piont, I didn't ask him what that was all about considering I was in too much pain. Also, I couldn't read the note anyway because it looked like a chicken wrote it.

When I saw the counsellor, I gave her the note and she

explained that if I wanted to, I could sign up with the centre for access and disabilty office in the college. Right away I got defensive and said, "Oh my God. I can't do that. I don't have a disability." I thought, 'What would people think of me if I used that service?' She waited for me to calm down and explained that cluster headaches are triggered by stress and that if I did sign up in the disability office I could get extra benefits, like ongoing support from college disability consultants, free tutoring to help with my homework, learning strategy training to help me study for tests, training in the use of specialized computer technology, advice and mentoring, and classroom and test accommodations, which would allow me to do all my tests in the testing centre, where I could book a private room. They also offered to give me a chance to apply for a bursary so I could see a psychologist to get an up-to-date educational and psychological assessment done, because I kept saying I was having a hard time with my English while writing an essay.

I saw a psychologist after a period of time and when I went to see him, I felt nervous and unsure of what to expect when walking through his front door. I thought if people saw me walking into his office, they would think I was nuts or something. I noticed that the door wasn't just for the psychologist, but it was for a driving school, too. So, when I left I grabbed something with the driving school's picture on it and pretended I was reading it until I got around the corner, where I dumped it in the garbage.

I walked into the office and looked around and didn't see a secretary or anyone else. I could only hear a man with a deep voice talking on the phone, so I sat in the office trying to picture what this psychologist would look like, and all I could see in my mind was an image of Albert Einstein with his fuzzy, grey hair and brown moustache, old looking. Then, for about five minutes before he came out to get me, I was looking at the way the office looked. It looked like the building was old. It had wood panelling on the walls, and the pictures in the office looked like they from the 1950s or so. When the psychologist came out, I realized I was totally wrong in the way I pictured him. He was tall, had brown hair (not fuzzy), was in his early 50s and had a soft handshake as he introduced himself to me with his deep voice. The psychologist then asked me to come in and told me the visit would take about five hours and that I would have to come back in the morning for another three to four hours to complete the assessment. Once he had time to go over all off the stuff, which would take two to three weeks, he would ask the counsellors at the college to make an appointment with me so he could go over everything he'd learned.

While in the office with him, I felt weird because he would get me to do things that a young child would enjoy, like drawing a picture, playing with blocks, counting and looking at pictures, and when he took them away, I had to tell him what I saw. I knew it was an educational test for which the psychologist had to start from kindergarten and climb up because he wanted to evaluate what level my learning was at. That night when I walked home, all I could feel going through my body was an overwhelming feeling of joy. For some reason, I felt like so happy, as though something was lifted off my body. The next day, I felt more confident about being there. I felt like I was accomplishing something, even though the psychologist was analyzing me the whole time.

When I received an email about two and a half weeks later, I really felt scared because the counsellor and psychologist both wanted to make an appointment to see me at the college to go through his assessment. I didn't know what to think, so I thought the worst. I thought they'd say I couldn't stay in the college and my English wasn't good enough to do the work. While waiting for my turn to see the psychologist, I saw another student come out of the office, crying and seeming very upset. So, once again, I felt I should just take off and forget college. As nervous as I was, my feet wouldn't let me go and when they came out and called me to come in, I had so many different thoughts going through my head, and I was speechless. The psychologist introduced himself again and then handed me his assessment, which I had no clue how to read because it kept mentioning "percentiles." He took an hour to go over the assessment with me and gave me the offer of coming to see either him or one of the counsellors at the college to explain it further, as I might not have been able to digest it all that day.

The psychologist said I had a learning disability that would keep me from doing well in college unless I got certain assistance to help guide me. The assessment included the following: My performance IQ indicated my intelligence was stronger via nonverbal materials, like pictures and visual materials; my language skills and short-term auditory memory were not as strong; my visual-motor speed skills were within normal limits; my visual memory was stronger than my auditory memory; when it came to reading and written expression, my academic skills were at the elementary grade level, which was lower than would be expected based on my abilities. All this information put together meant I had a learning disorder.

I was told that as long as I was willing to use certain services at the college, I could make it through and graduate. Here are some of the services that I am using are: asking my instructor(s) for extra time to complete assignments; tutoring to help understand the assignments clearly; using the testing centre to do all tests unless given a take-home test; the college gave me a bursary to help buy a computer with Dragon (software that helps turn my voice to text in Word 2007, three times faster than I could type) and Kurzweil. (A comprehensive reading, writing and learning software solution for any struggling reader, including individuals with learning difficulties). I was also informed that I could reduce my course load to 40%, the lowest limit one is allowed to have while still receiving funding from the Ontario Student Assistance Program.

When I left that office, I could understand why the young girl was crying and very upset, because when I came out of the room, I was emotionally lost. I didn't know if I wanted to cry or scream, so all I did was sit in a room full of people I knew and more or less I just said nothing and tried to digest what was said. It was a week or so later that I decided to make an appointment to see the counsellor on a regular basis. She knows how to read those psycho-educational reports. So I felt a bit better going in to see her and asking her to explain what this all really meant. She read it to me and explained everything by using visual maps. I felt weird when we were talking about my learning disorder, but I accepted the situation and asked what I should do next. She suggested that I sign up in the Centre for Access as a student with a disability so I could use all the equipment and services to help make it through college. I didn't like the fact that I had to get extra help or be classified with a learning disorder, but I wanted to make sure I passed all my classes. So, if using the services could help me, I was willing to do it. Over time, I met many people (who I never would have predicted needed help) who came into the Centre for Access. That made me feel like I wasn't alone anymore.

In college, I had to give presentations in front of the class, and I'd really get nervous, as though I had performance anxiety. (Anxiety involves an intense emotional reaction brought on by anticipation of future problems.) But everyone I talk to says, "Wow. You were nervous? I would have never known." I love the feeling when I get compliments, as it makes me want to try even harder next time.

I found that when I first started at Georgian College, I didn't really have a good view of my future, but now that I know I could get the help needed to achieve any goals I intended to. I studied at a slower pace and I achieve good grades. I even got on the dean's list three times in two years. With all the help I have been receiving, I can proudly say I finished the social service worker program in December 2010 and have entered the bachelor of social work program at Lakehead University in January 2011.

Chapter 11

Summary

There was a time when I was drinking in some bushes. I thought that life had really dealt me the wrong cards. Sometimes when feeling sorry for myself, I would look at my situation of me being homeless, broke, hungry and having only a few friends (drunks) to talk to. I didn't feel like I belonged and really didn't feel there was anything to be proud of, yet at the same time, for a long, long time, I did nothing to change the way I was living.

Today, I wouldn't change my worst days in recovery for my best days while using drugs or alcohol, because I feel through these last five years, plus in recovery, I have learned so much about why I was doing all the things I did and I learned how to handle or accept each emotion as they come so I don't overreact. If I don't understand the emotion I am feeling, I have the option today to talk to someone about it. I can identify and learn how to properly use it. I am so grateful to the people who took a chance to help empower me to overcome all the tough times and become the person I am today.

When looking at my past, through my own eyes today, I am stunned to see the difference in the paths I chose. Although they are quite different in their colour, they are the same in many ways. I still have lots of people around me who support and encourage me. My drug of choice now is school. I still stay up all night, but I'm usually volunteering at a crisis hotline or studying for an exam. My struggles include trying to figure out how to help people help themselves and my assaultive behaviour now comes from hugging someone too hard.

Although I went through a lot of emotional, physical and mental pain, I believe now that I wouldn't change a thing about my past because this has made me a stronger, wiser person, and I'm very proud of the person I am today. I hope sharing my story will help others get off the rough road they're on and know there are other roads to choose. Additionally, I realize that I still have a lot of learning to do, and I'm willing to learn from other people's mistakes, as I am not going to live long enough to make them all myself.

I have created an email address to hear from people who read this book and I'd like to know how my story has helped you through your tough times.
The email is theres_moore_to_life@live.ca.

I look forward to hearing from you,
Robert Moore

Appendix

Achievements

I am very proud of all of my achievements. I've listed them here:

I might have achieved a lot of small goals, but as soon as I achieve a goal I am going for, I make a commitment without hesitation to achieve another. I found that I didn't have to work all alone while making these goals a reality and come to life. I have on many occasions seen other people to help me focus on these goals, like my anger management and addictions counsellors and people at Georgian College's Ontario Student Assistance Program office, as they handle all the awards that come through the college.

Awards & Bursaries

I have won a lot of awards and thousands of dollars over the last few years. This helped me pay off some of the debt I accumulated over time. Here are some of the awards I have achieved in the last five years while I was in school, volunteering and focusing on achieving another goal.

September 1, 2009 I established a financial award at Georgian College, the Robert Moore Award.
Orillia Power Corporation Undergrad Achievement Award (Georgian College, April 2010)
Ontario First Generation Bursary (Georgian College, March

2010)

Simcoe College Foundation Award (Georgian College, March 2009)

Georgian College bursaries provide $750 each year to help me out financially. This was put towards my second semester.

Courage to Come Back Award (Centre for Addictions and Mental Health Foundation, 2007)

Lieutenant Governor's Community Volunteer Award for Students and the college community bursary (the Orillia Learning Centre, June 2007)

Ontario Secondary School Diploma, (June 2007)

Sobriety since September 7, 2005 (free from drugs and alcohol)

Certificates

October 23, 2010: I received a certificate for tutoring (Laubach Literacy Ontario)

Recognition of participation for A Night in the Cold to raise awareness of homelessness (October 2008)

Ontario Youth Apprenticeship Program presentation (February 2007)

Service Excellence participation (March 2007)

Dress for Success Seminar certificate (March 2007)